Decorative Art
and Modern Interiors

Decorative Art
and Modern Interiors 1977

Volume 66 Edited by Maria Schofield

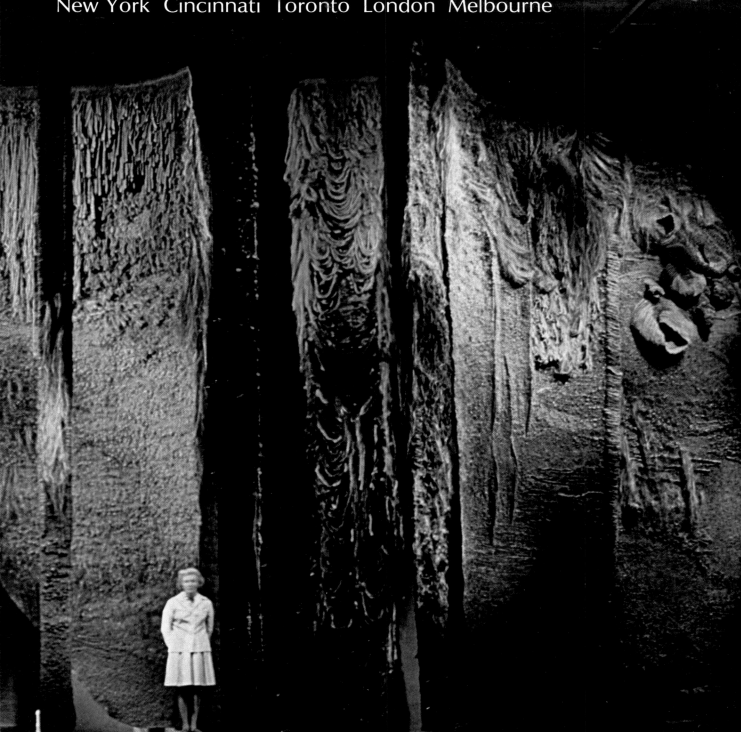

Studio Vista
London

Van Nostrand Reinhold Company
New York Cincinnati Toronto London Melbourne

Cover
The entrance hall in 'An
Apartment for a Collector of
Modern Art in Rome, Italy'.
Architects: Giorgio Pes and
Roberto Federici (front). A detail
from 'Studio for a Stage Designer
in Rome, Italy'
Architect: Pier Luigi Pizzi (back)
Photography by
Carla de Benedetti

Title page

1 – 'Relief in Space'; a 200 sq. m.
environmental textile structure
for the reception room of a State
Building in 's Hertogenbosch,
Holland
Made by Magdalena Abacanowicz
Photography by Virginia West

A Studio Vista book publication by
Cassell & Collier Macmillan Publishers Ltd,
35 Red Lion Square, London WC1 4SG
and at Sydney, Auckland, Johannesburg
an affiliate of
Macmillan Publishing Co Inc
New York

Copyright © Studio Vista 1977
First published in 1977

Published in 1977 by
Van Nostrand Reinhold Company
A division of Litton Educational Publishing, Inc
450 West 33rd Street, New York, NY 10001, USA

Van Nostrand Reinhold Limited
1410 Birchmount Road
Scarborough, Ontario M1P 2E7, Canada

Library of Congress Cataloging in Publication Data
Main entry under title:
Decorative art and modern interiors, 1977.
    1. Art, Decorative.   2. Interior decoration.
I. Schofield, Maria.
NK1390.D4   1977   745.4'44   76-29529
U.S. ISBN 0-442-27423-8
U.K. ISBN 0 289 70729.9

Designed by Angus Hamilton
Set in Monophoto Optima 10 on 11 pt by
Tradespools Ltd, Frome, Somerset
Separations by Colorlito, Milano, Italy
Printed and bound in Italy by Amilcare Pizzi SpA, Milano
16 15 14 13 12 11 10 9 8 7 6 5 4 3 2 1

Contents

Acknowledgements

The Editor wishes to thank those manufacturers
and designers who supplied photographs for
reproduction and especially the Museum of
Modern Art, Kyoto, The Renwick Gallery of the
Smithsonian Institution, Washington DC, the
Craft Advisory Committee and the British
Craft Centre, London, and Miss Carla Caccia,
Milan, for their valid support.

Introduction

'Art in Architecture' would appear to be a very presumptuous heading to a collection of interiors where people live their ordinary, everyday lives; and to a certain extent this is justifiably so. We often think of Art as something exclusive, the privilege of the few who can afford to spend their days visiting exhibitions, the theatre and the concert hall, go on pilgrimage to Greece and Italy, Japan and Mexico. As a corollary from this, we use the word *creative* to define activities that have an element of fantasy in them, as opposed to good plain, sensible ones. We even push the paradox to the extreme by distinguishing a 'creative' photographer, for example, who manipulates the negative film during the developing process to obtain special, *artistic* effects, from his cousin the 'industrial' photographer, who still has to do a lot of processing to put in evidence a certain characteristic of a machine. If successful, the latter is no lesser an artist than the former. We deem a sunset beautiful but a simple screw only functional; yet the spiral of an ordinary screw is beautiful when we forget for a moment its practical connotation. But our specialist demon tempts our timid minds into calling this 'Industrial Design' rather than 'Design', let alone ART. Perhaps then we might give some thought to the definition that Octavio Paz gave of Art, as being aesthetic *contemplation rather than use*. Everyone of us experiences the moment of contemplation, even during the busiest practical activity. It is this moment that makes us perceive the beauty that surrounds us. Whether in a museum, on a country walk, in an office, or at home, Art is part of our ordinary, everyday lives.

Following this guideline, the collection of twenty interiors included in this edition of 'Decorative Art' has been put together in an attempt to show some of the many ways that involve Art into Architecture. For instance, there are examples of architecture designed for specific art activities, such as the 'Concert Hall in Helsinki' and the 'Museum of Modern Art in Takasaki', the collaboration between artists and architects from the initial planning of a project,

as in the 'St Joseph Church in Geilenkirchen' and the 'Oulunkylä Church and Community Centre'; the conversion of a 19th century apartment that was in turn part of a free reconstruction of a Renaissance cloister; or the accidental discovery of a 19th century beam structure and how it inspired the inner architecture of a studio, as in 'A Studio for a Stage Designer in Rome'. Most awesome of all perhaps is the design of the 'Home for an Art Collector', conceived within the majestic architecture of a Roman palace of the XVII century. One daren't call this a conversion, with the implication of transformation the name suggests, such is the mastery that translates the Roman Baroque idiom into contemporary proportions that still retain the powerful scale and rhythm of the classic original.

Among the most recent projects, the 'Kresge College in Santa Cruz, University of California', evokes the grace and warmth of a mediterranean village through the advantage of a hill setting and the use of colour and graphics. 'The House with a Cantilever Roof in Kitakyushu' demonstrates the imaginative power that employs rigid, cold materials for a most flexible arrangement of interior spaces. And its counterpart in Italy, the 'Family House for a Doctor near Milan', proves that hard, geometrical shapes of steel and glass become alive when perceived by a sensitive mind.

A comparatively new approach to the age-old craft of weaving is examined by Virginia West in the special feature included in this edition. The author, who teaches and practises weaving, follows the course of events of the last twenty years, when painters and sculptors became interested in the physical properties of fibre and participated in the actual process of weaving, an activity that had in the past been considered either as an expression of folklore or as skilled labour employed in the manufacture of tapestries from cartoons designed by an artist. The degree of excellence and novelty reached in this art medium has not failed to attract the interest of both gallery owners and architects, and whenever possible examples of fibre structures especially commissioned for a particular interior have been illustrated and analysed. In other instances entire fibre environments have been shown; architecture in their own right such as Jagoda Buić's 'Of the Stone, Of the Sun, Of the Dream' or Olga de Amaral's 'Environment for the Town Hall at 's Hertogenbosch'. A review of two international textile exhibitions, the '7ᵉ Biennale Internationale de la Tapisserie' in Lausanne, 1975, and the '2nd International Exhibition of Miniature Textiles' organized in July 1976 by the British Crafts Centre, in London, completes an account of 'The Art of Fibre.'

The last part of the book concerns in particular craft work produced either in small workshops; or in cooperatives where craftsmen can hire workshop space and share equipment; or even in the spare room in the craftsman's own home. Whatever the social or economic reasons responsible for this, the standard of work is so high that museums have begun to take notice. 'Craft Multiples', an exhibition organized by the Renwick Gallery of the National Collection of Fine Arts, Smithsonian Institution, was on show in Washington DC from July 1975 till February 1976, and is currently travelling the United States on a tour that will go on till the end of March 1979. In the words of Lloyd E Herman, Director of the Renwick Gallery, the originating idea of the exhibition was 'to match the attention usually given to the artist-craftsman who makes unique objects by mounting an exhibition of well-designed and well-made craft works produced in multiples of at least ten'. A collection of 133 objects made by 126 craftsmen, varying in size, purpose and cost from a full-scale buggy to a set of Christmas ornaments of baked salt dough 2″ to 3″ tall, brought to the notice of an enthusiastic public a wide range of different craft techniques, working methods, and, most important of all perhaps, life-styles.

In June 1976 the Crafts Advisory Committee in London staged 'Showbusiness', its first 'commercial' exhibition, with the purpose of drawing people's attention to the retail outlets selling and dealing in the work of British artist-craftsmen. Ten craft galleries, selected throughout the country, put on display beautiful pieces by weavers, glassblowers, potters, jewellers, woodturners and printmakers; some lesser known craftsmen's work was exhibited next to unique pieces by others whose work is included in many museum collections of the world.

Such events are bound to provoke reverberations that sooner or later, given the current economic recession, will affect the market place. Some concerns have already had to bow out of the scene, others might have to follow; the reduced participation in international trade fairs bears witness to this. The more healthy survivors will continue to turn material restrictions to advantage. As Ludwig Schaffrath stated during a public lecture on stained glass, given to the Royal Society of Arts in June 1975, '. . . there is nothing like a shortage of funds to refine design. It is an excellent challenge and in general it spurs creativity.' Quality of industrial production will have to improve to match the standard of excellence and dedication of an increasing number of craftsmen and satisfy a more aesthetically aware public.

Maria Schofield

Art in Architecture

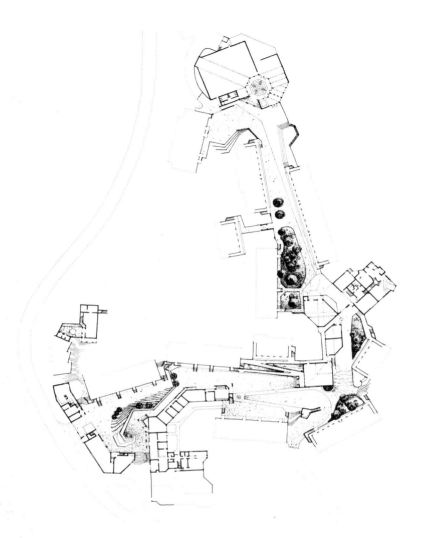

Kresge College in Santa Cruz University of California

The University of California campuses are vast places: Berkeley has 27,000 students, Santa Barbara, among the smaller ones, counts as many as 9,000. Santa Cruz was conceived as a collection of individual colleges within a university campus, as a solution to the impersonal problem created by sheer number.

Kresge College was commissioned by a body comprising students and faculty members whose primary requirement was a non-institutional alternative to the usual classroom and residential designs often found in universities. State and Federal resources, plus

a gift from the Kresge family, provided funds for a residential college with accommodation for 325 of its 650 students.

The site, a densely wooded hill-top, overlooks Monterey Bay. Two sides are precipitous, the third slopes gently to the south. At the bottom of this slope a tight pedestrian street rises 45 ft from the access area (bottom left in plan) to the octagon at the top of the hill. The buildings arranged alongside the street have a central core flanked by an outer 'shell' punctured by a rhythmical sequence of irregular openings; this

3 – Main gate and commuter
student facilities

4 – The laundry and, to the
right, a residential block

5 – The middle courtyard, with
laundry to the left, dormitory in
centre and telephone arch
facing laundry

provides an intermediate traffic area flowing onto the street which thus becomes a centre for the college; a place where people meet as in the street of a Mediterranean village. This, the 'inside' of the college, is all white, though strikingly marked with primary colours to accentuate important landmarks. The exterior, on the forest side, is sienna brown. Structures for special functions act as markers in strategic positions along the street. The octagonal court at the upper end provides an entry to the town hall space and restaurant. The library has a two-storey gateway. The laundry, a symbolic town watering hole, is endowed with a triumphal arch, echoed across

the space of the middle plaza by a raised podium, situated so as to conceal the trash box. Other important services, such as telephone booths, are emphasized as commentary on the importance of communications in student and faculty life.

The accommodation is planned in three different ways. The apartments contain a sleeping space for four people plus a combined kitchen, dining and living room. On the lower floor the sleeping space is divided into two double bedrooms facing out toward the privacy of the forest. The upper units have the advantage of extra ceiling height, and in these

8 – A student double room; the top bed rests on Palaset containers, designed by Ristomatti Ratia for Treston Oy Finland

9 – Faculty common room

10 – General view of the library, with steps to full height window on the forest side

11 – A secluded corner in the library

12 – View of staircase; note how the inner walls are also punctured by openings

13 – The assembly hall

14 – The fountain near the cooperative store and coffee house at topmost corner on plan

sleeping space is left for sub-division by the occupant's furniture. These apartments provide an answer to those who wish the more unstructured life of off-campus living.

A second residential unit is the dormitory suite. Two double rooms and four single rooms are arranged along an exterior balcony, in preference to the usual double-loaded corridor systems. Entry to all rooms is from the street side. Instead of combining all the student common space into one or two rooms, each dormitory has its own small living room and kitchenette. The result is rather like a motel.

The last residential system was designed for the more resourceful individual. Throughout the University, students tend to move from the campus to live in old Victorian houses in downtown Santa Cruz or little redwood summer shacks in the surrounding mountains. Four units for eight people were built as an 'on campus' alternative. Each unit provides the shell of the space, toilet facilities and kitchen. The occupants, on moving in, decide on how to subdivide the space and negotiate with the University Fire Marshal for approval. They are given materials (wood and sheetrock) and use of the college tools to construct their own living quarters. In choosing the furniture,

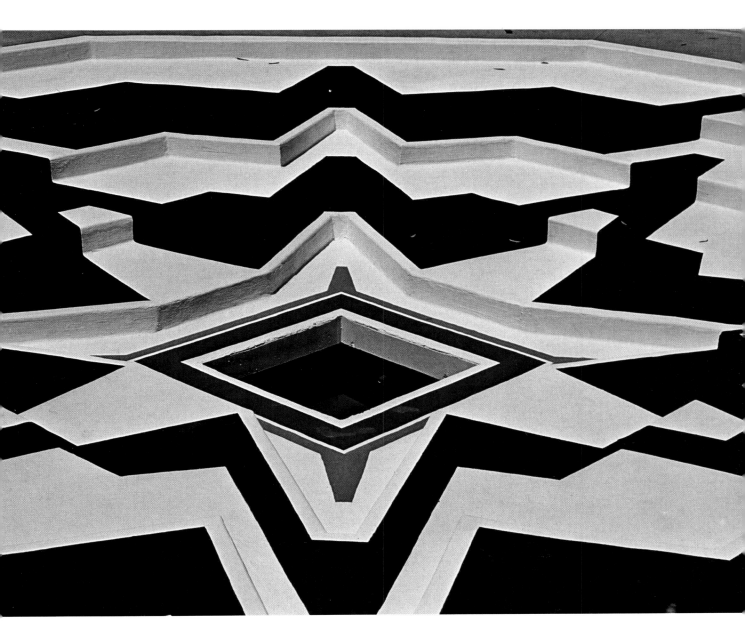

quality and maximum flexibility of use were of primary importance. The Finnish 'Palaset' plastic cube system, designed by Ristomatti Ratia, was eventually selected. Each student was given sixteen $13\frac{1}{2}''$ cubes, a desk top, a bed board, foam mattress and a director's chair, and left to his own resources.

Classroom furnishing ranges from the traditional to beech chairs on the floor or pillows on raised platforms. The student common became a 'crash pad' for commuters and the faculty common turned into a small formal living room for the entire college community. The library was looked upon as a space where one could

quietly read or work either at a desk or sprawled onto the floor. A fireplace provided an intimate focus and a large sunken bay looks out into the redwoods.

The effect of the college is one of an outdoor living room (the street) with the personal domain (student rooms) opening onto it. Semi-public spaces, classrooms, laundry, craft space, library, are extensions of the public street and are informal places for the exchange of ideas. Kresge's philosophy is that education takes place on all levels at all times and that stimulating environments are an asset to the process of learning.

15 – The house under construction, showing the service core and the H-profile steel girders supporting the concrete roof.

16 – Isometric plan

1 Entrance
2 Living/dining
3 Kitchen
4 Bathroom
5 Bedroom

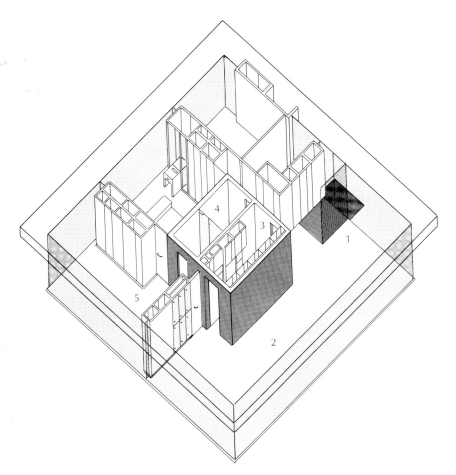

The House with a Cantilever Roof in Kitakyushu, Japan

At the time of writing this article the 'House with a Cantilever Roof' is without replica; a 'unique piece', as a proud craftsman would be eager to point out. The concept however was to design a 'universal' house that could be produced in series; a house for as many occupants as its generously proportioned roof would shelter, resembling in concept a huge tree with a wide spreading crown.

The only pre-determined components of such a house are a steel and concrete deep central core, a platform, and a cantilever roof. The 'hard' core contains main services: kitchen, bathroom and installations; around it, a 'soft' free open space can be sub-divided into living, study, sleeping areas by arranging at will the movable, floor-to-ceiling containers that also function as partition walls. The whole interior is encased with glass in the example illustrated here, but other materials could be used equally well.

The plan is clearly divided into day and night areas, respectively to left and right of the service core. The kitchen is a rectangular room, with cupboards and equipment ranged along its longer sides; one door opens to dining, the other to entrance/living area, so that traffic is flowing directly from service to entertainment. Bedrooms can be reached both

17 – The entertainment area as seen from entrance. Note how total privacy is obtained by using vertical blinds

18 – Dining area: view over city

19 – The L-shaped living/dining space; to the right is the bathroom/kitchen unit

from the main entrance, via a corridor, and through a door from dining to the master bedroom. The bath is divided by a glass partition and communicates with the master bedroom at its shower/tub end. See the isometric plan.

The decoration is very simple throughout: white acrylic paint for ceiling and container/partitions; oatmeal carpet for entertainment space and bedrooms; wood, marble. Two granite slabs supported by thick plate glass

function as dining and coffee tables; their precise, hard lines are balanced by the elegant curves of Mies van der Rohe chairs and Castiglioni floor lamp; sofa and armchairs of maroon suède were designed by Shoei Yoh.

An easily maintained, flexible universal house. Totally unorthodox in concept, so far as Japanese building traditions go. But then, in the words of its architect, 'since pre-historic times, and even now, it's still nice to rest under a big tree'.

20 – Two views of the bathroom, showing double doors and glass partition. Glass shelves are glued to the partition; the stainless steel tube between shower and wash basin is a roof drain

21 – Kitchen; containers under working surfaces can be used as trolleys. On the floor, a trap door leads to a basement storage area

22 – Master bedroom; containers serve as room dividers and can easily be arranged in different ways; note how space is ingeniously utilized in detail. All partitions were made to order, designed by Shoei Yoh

23 – View from the garden at night

Architect: Angelo Cortesi

Photography by Giovanna dal Magro and Gianni Berengo-Gardin

24 – Plan showing the
arrangement of the basic blocks

25 – Outside view

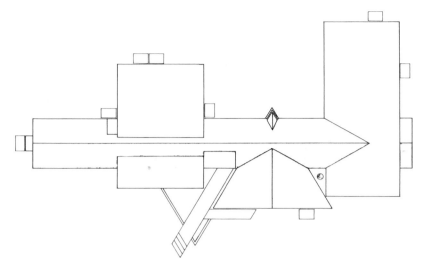

A Family House for a Doctor near Milan, Italy

There is a conceptual relationship between this house and Arata Isozaki's Museum in that its plan has an immediately recognizable geometrical formula. But the similarity ends there. In contrast with the Museum, where the cube frame is multiplied in accordance with its own rhythm, Cortesi's basic idea, binary in concept, is composed of a triangle and a rectangle. The juxtaposition of these two shapes intersecting each other, generating tensions that must be solved, leads eventually to a different type of harmony : a harmony through discord. The rectangular 'blocks' are cut on the slant, elevations have triangular sections; the conflicting shapes fuse together.

That Cortesi's idea should be embodied in a dwelling house is daring, since to express it fully, cold, unwielding materials had to be used inside and out; one does in effect flinch at the prospect of walking on a stainless steel floor. Yet a young doctor in general practice and his family live and work in this 'difficult' house on the outskirts of Milan. These primary forms that run into each other, then reassert their own identity, contain spaces that are unusual but undeniably stimulating. The large expanse of glass abolishes boundaries, introduces the landscape in the interior. Light creates unsuspected relationships. All tends to give the impression of a wider area than the

26 – Plan of interior

1 Entrance
2 Gallery
3 Living
4 Surgery
5 Kitchen
6 Dining
7 Storage
8 Bedroom
9 Bathroom
10 Dressing room

27 – View from the gallery; to
the left is the entrance door,
with living area beyond; to the
right is a wedge-shaped corner
nicknamed 'il pensatoio' (the
think-tank)

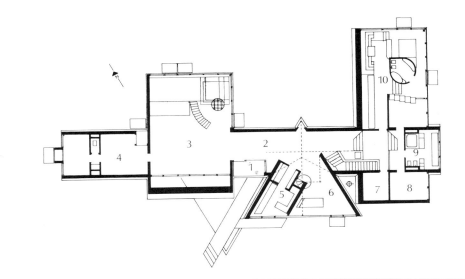

actual 300 sq m covered. Further, the logic of this rigorous architectural idiom contains its own reward in that it produces spaces of unique character, 'adopted' by members of the family as their preferred ones.

The house is planned as three main blocks intersected by a long gallery that has an independent waiting room and surgery at its north-western end. A door leads to the wedge-shaped living area on two levels; here the north wall is entirely made of rectangular panes of glass. The second block is an irregular pyramid merging with the gallery; it faces south with a triangular glazed front and contains kitchen and dining area. The third block is another wedge-shaped rectangle for the night area. Although the gallery continues structurally through this part, its presence is disguised by a change in level that in one operation secures privacy for the bedrooms, without an actual separating wall, and provides underfloor storage space. Furniture is mostly built-in, designed by the architect. The main structure is stainless steel on concrete block. Finishes are white paint, plastic laminates, exposed concrete slabs, stainless steel.

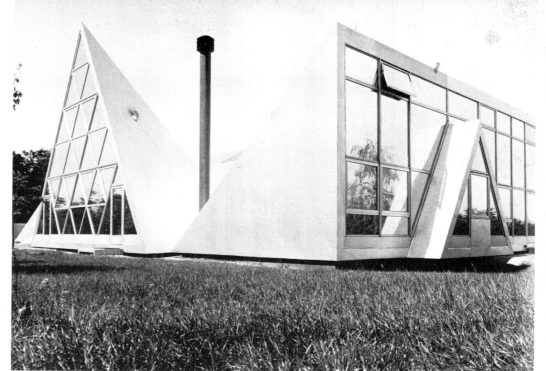

28 – General view of the living area, with concrete steps leading to upper level

29 – A corner in the living area; a segmented sphere fireplace, with its articulated steel flue, rests on a conversation pit under the upper level

30 – Outside view; to the right is the bathroom wall, made of two-way mirror

31 – Detail of bathroom.

32 – Late afternoon sun on the north elevation. View across frozen lake

33 – Main entrance

Finlandia Hall, Helsinki, Finland

Finlandia Hall was built as the first stage of a complex, long term development that will give Helsinki a new civic centre, approached by a net of motorways built over the old railway tracks. The centre will be connected to a system of underground traffic streets and large parking areas covered by a terraced open space at the head of Lake Töölö. Seen in this context, the massive scale of the building becomes easier to understand. Besides, the monumental character of the architecture is never overwhelming; the structure is integrated in the cityscape in such a way that most of its volume is below street level because the site

slopes down to the water's edge and a complete view of the building is only possible at a distance, across the lake.

Within a space totalling 150,000 sq ft of floor areas, on four levels, there are a concert/congress hall for 1,750 people, a smaller chamber music hall for 350, three 100-seat conference rooms and 20 smaller meeting rooms of varying sizes that double as rehearsal, practice and study rooms for musicians. In addition there are administrative offices, restaurants and an information centre. An impressive communication network links all

34 – Looking from chamber music foyer to main hall foyer

35 – View of main foyer from entrance

Overpage
36 – The main concert hall

parts of the building; a three-channel, closed-circuit television system allows various functions to be monitored in other areas; activities in the main hall can be simultaneously projected on a large screen in the chamber music hall, thus increasing the audience capacity by 350. Both music halls and all conference rooms are fitted with simultaneous interpreting equipment for six languages. In the main concert hall, sections of the stage can be hydraulically raised or lowered into various combinations. The aspect of the building gives immediately a feeling of occasion, heightened by the quality of materials

37 – Detail of ceiling in main hall

38 – The chamber music hall

employed and by an exceptional degree of fine workmanship. On the outside, polished Carrara marble contrasts with polished and rough areas of local black granite. In the interior, the choice of surface materials depends on the function of each area. The heavily used main entrance foyer is treated with hard wearing travertine (floors and stairs), marble-faced walls, easily maintained ceramic tiles to protect the columns. As one climbs to the upper level foyers, materials become softer; some walls and columns are of white painted plaster, floors are carpeted in pale grey.

39 – Looking from the south-east towards main auditorium tower; note in centre the projected stair from main auditorium, interrupting the uniform rhythm of the windows

The chamber music hall has walls partially covered with painted wooden panels, and redwood lines the acoustical floating baffles hanging from the ceiling. In the main hall, the walls are painted white and contrast with the dark blue wooden acoustic panels and with the marble-faced balconies. Behind the ceiling grilles there is a large interstitial space, reinforced by steel trusses, where sliding steel hatches can be opened or closed individually to tune the hall below – a long, controversial process that will need satisfy both the wishes for a 'soft' acoustic, traditionally associated with classic concert performances, and the

demands of a younger generation of concert-goers whose ears are attuned to the crispness of high fidelity reproductions.

The whole design idea is expressed in every detail, from the highly specialized organ installation to the furniture, light fixtures, wood and metal grilles, handrails (made of brass wrapped in leather), even the door pulls. This is a complete synthesis of form, only possible when a single mind, such as Aalto's is in control of every aspect of a project.

Architect: Building Design Partnership
Partner: N Keith Scott

Photography by John Mills

A School in Preston, England

40 – General view from the south

A mixed five form entry secondary school for 720 children was to be built just outside the Lancashire town of Preston. The 25 acres site had a distinct rural character, with access from the north on level ground, then stepping down very sharply towards the south boundary into a valley with a stream flowing westwards. After exhaustive study it was decided to build on the slope, reserving the level area for playing fields. This meant a longer, more expensive access road but offered the advantage that the school buildings could be broken down into small units, a logical solution to the client's desire that the departments

within the school should be clearly divided. An architectural link would connect the units and negotiate the difference in levels. Problems of costly drainage were solved by creating numerous pools which receive all the top water from two main blocks; this also avoids below ground drainage other than the outlet from the pools and affords recreational and teaching facilities, particularly appreciated by the natural sciences students.

The main entrance, on the western side of the basic block, is dominated by a large stained glass window by William Mitchell. Throughout

26

41 – Entrance hall; to the left is the stained window by William Mitchell

42 – The assembly hall

43 – The main restaurant

44 – One of the workshops

45, 46 – The central circulation area in the Technical Studies block

the interior there is an evident concern to echo the outside architecture, as for example in the design of the suspended ceiling in the assembly hall and in the use of the same materials : brick, copper, wood.

The star-shaped technical unit was designed to minimize circulation area and at the same time give a feeling of space. Starting from the fact that the most economical pattern to gain access to a group of rooms is a circle, various architectural possibilities were explored and it was eventually discovered that, provided

47 – The smaller oval hall

48 – View of Technical Studies
block and senior playground
from the south-west

the client would accept rather unusually
shaped storerooms, all the six classrooms
could be rectangular, the best shape for
teaching purposes. This scheme also proved
cheaper to build and the savings were
employed to obtain a higher quality of finish.
The tall central tower is also a most suitable
setting for exhibitions of wood and metalwork
made by the children.

The dining room has no less than five eating
spaces, including a gallery, main restaurant,
a coffee bar and a smaller oval hall built outside
the main building.

Architects: Dufau et Briaudet
Interior Designer: Michel Boyer

Photography by Gerrard Guillat

The Town Hall in Créteil, France

49 – General view; the wide-angle lens emphasizes the round mass of the building

Créteil was, about thirty years ago, a rural community of 12,000 inhabitants. It is today part of a vast project of development in the Paris region, realized by a team of urbanists, architects, engineers, landscape and interior designers, artists – a cooperation rarely found on a more modest scale. The new town of nearly 100,000 inhabitants is rapidly changing into an important commercial and industrial centre, with numerous factories; in the vicinity, a landscaped regional park including an artificial lake is being built.

The Town Hall is a distinctive landmark, with its low circular building devoted to public ceremonial spaces and the cylindrical tower for the administrative offices. At the top of this tower are the Mayor's private offices and reception rooms.

In harmony with the general plan, radiating from the centre, the interior design follows the curving walls, adopts the circular shape for the raised platforms of the ceremonial rooms, the design of the suspended ceiling

50 – The reception hall, at
ground floor level. The enquiry
desk rests on a large blue
circular carpet

51 – The stairs of laminated wood, by Pierre Dufau, leading to the main reception hall dominated by the tapestry designed by Vasarely

and the fitted furniture in the Mayor's office. Very subtle elements are however introduced to avoid the monotony of reiteration; as an example, the wooden wall panels in the principal reception hall are stained matt and lacquered black, with an effect of matt and shining alternating areas. Focal points are provided by numerous art pieces – a striking hanging designed by Vasarely among them. Large murals and decorative panels on sliding doors by the painter Jean-Paul Derive contribute dynamism to these opulent, though generally neutral spaces.

52, 53 – Overall view of
Wedding Hall and detail
showing the Mayor's desk.

54 – The Mayor's private office
has black lacquered panels
concealing files and official
records. On the background a
decorative multicoloured mural
by Jean-Paul Derive. Seating is
of natural leather by Cini Boeri
for Knoll International and
Airborne. Rust coloured carpet

55 – At one end of the Mayor's
office, a sliding door opens onto
a private dining room, which
in turn leads to the Council
Meeting Room. Tables are
designed by Michel Boyer and are
of wood stained black resting on
a polished aluminium base.
Pollock chairs upholstered
green complete the furnishings.

56 – Plan

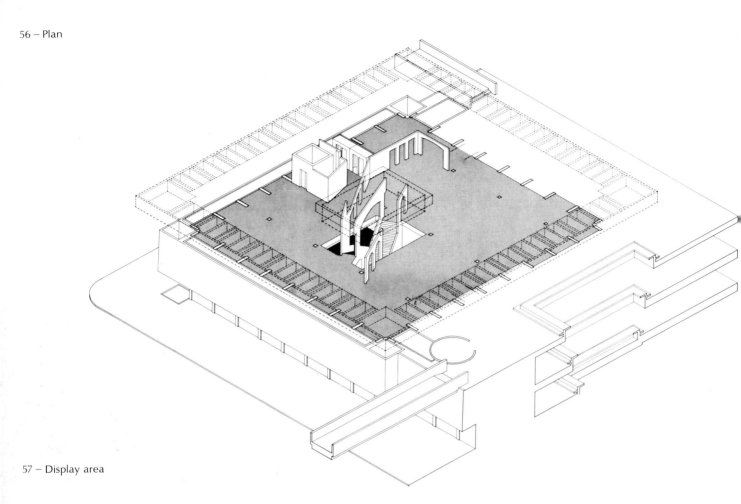

57 – Display area

'Design Research', a Department Store in San Francisco, California

The space reserved for commercial use in the new Embarcadero Centre, built by John Portman in San Francisco, was contained in a heavy structural grid of concrete on the north side of the Security Pacific Tower. When Design Research decided to open another store in San Francisco, they asked William Turnbull, well known for his imaginative approach, to design the interior.

Stair circulation and daylight were the basic elements used to solve what the architect describes as the 'paradoxes' found in dealing with a previously defined structure on a poor site. The existing 18 by 28 ft roof was replaced by a skylight; the two-storey space was linked by double stairs on the diagonal, giving access on two levels. Above these, free-standing arches frame the entire space, their various sizes and shapes evoking 'the poetic idiosyncrasies of Victorian San Francisco houses'; they are outlined by neon tubing, to emphasize the independence of the architectural whole from its outer 'container'.

58 – Stairs to upper level

59 – Detail of staircase

60 – View from lower level
showing skylight above.

Over the display area, fluorescent ceiling
fixtures are again set diagonally and exposed
to view together with pipes, ducts and wires,
usually hidden by a false ceiling, above a lattice
of aluminium studs. Wooden block floor,
simple racks and containers, plants hanging
from ceiling, standing at corners and on
furniture, set off ideally the lively merchandise
that inspired William Turnbull and his
colleagues this vibrant and stimulating
environment.

61 – Exterior view

A Studio for a Sculptor in Tokyo, Japan

When planning this building the architect followed two guidelines. The first reflected his belief that the environment should become an active, working factor in relation to the new building. In this case the environment consists of crowded wooden houses, typical of a Japanese residential area, and nearby there is a railway. Paradoxically, in trying to apply his convictions to the interior, the architect used glass extensively so as to invite the outer view, and even the noise of passing electric trains, directly into the rooms.

The second factor was the architect's long-nurtured concept of the 'box in a box' shape. Here one solid cubic box is contained by a larger, transparent, cube. The building is the studio of a sculptor as well as a gallery, so the inner shape has been devised for the display of art pieces and for work sessions. Occasionally the whole space becomes a salon for receiving friends and associates.

As an architectural idea this project is very exciting and should work well; provided of course that the social problems deriving from living in a glass house surrounded by wooden ones could be solved equally well.

62 – Interior, upper level

63 – Isometric plan
64 – Detail of display area

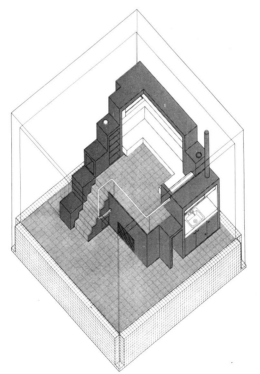

An Artist's Studio at Oberwang, Austria

The building of a motorway brought new life to the quiet Wangau river valley, where the gothic church of St Conrad lies surrounded by woods, meadows, gentle slopes. Nearby, in harmonious contrast with the old church, is the studio home of the artist.

Three cubes, constructed with stepped walls that follows closely the undulations of the terrain, are grouped around an inner courtyard. Two studios and a garage are arranged in the three units according to the function of the spaces, the necessities of lighting and the desire to look towards the little church and over the open country. The main parts of the

building intersect each other, giving a new variation to the traditional shape of the roof. This plan also allows the development of an internal upper level, used as gallery and library.

The architects believe that, for an artist, private life and work are directly related. To express this in architectural terms, spaces flow into each other, become stronger as one progresses from the small anteroom to the first studio, partly covered by the gallery, to the second larger studio which becomes a meeting place for the artist and her friends, particularly during the annual festival of poetry readings and organ recitals held in the church. At the

66 – Detail of one of the studios

69 – View from the inner courtyard to the main part of the
house, with entrance to the
right

67 – View from the larger studio
towards the upper gallery

68 – Detail of the gallery

same time the need for peace and meditation
is recognized and expressed in the unifying use
of simple building materials. Outside and inside
walls are exposed Lecabeton (concrete slabs
incorporating plastic pellets, of excellent
insulating and acoustic properties). The under-
side of the roof, ceilings and gallery are pine;
floors are reddish brown quarry tiles. Furniture
is minimal: simple chairs painted blue or red,
an old chest, an easel, a large trestle table.
The sleeping area is an alcove barely 2m × 2m
at the end of the gallery, with a view towards
the church and over the open countryside.

Architect: Keith Garbett
Interior Designer: Alan Boyce

Photography by Richard Einzig

70 – Outside view; to the left of the entrance porch is the north-facing wall of the new extension

A Conversion in Cambridgeshire, England

In Rampton High Street, opposite the church, stands the former village school; a two-storey hall of local brick with a steep slate roof. At one end there was an entrance porch, at the other a brick barrel-vaulted store, older than the main building, that was thought once to have contained the local jail. Opened as a National School in 1845 it functioned intermittently until 1964, when the school closed down and the building lay empty until Alan Boyce, an industrial designer, started restoration and conversion work in 1971. It has now become Alan Boyce's family home.

Although not listed as a building of special interest, its strong character appealed both to the owner and to the architect, who decided to preserve the original appearance as far as possible. The shape of the three exposed street sides was retained and restored, limiting the change only to the function of the existing additions; the porch became a larder and the jail the main entrance. The back elevation however was considerably altered to include a new extension and the addition of a fully glazed dormer window that reaches below and gives light to the ground floor and to a new gallery.

The interior design was planned jointly by owner and architect, and much of the finishings were executed by Alan Boyce himself. One

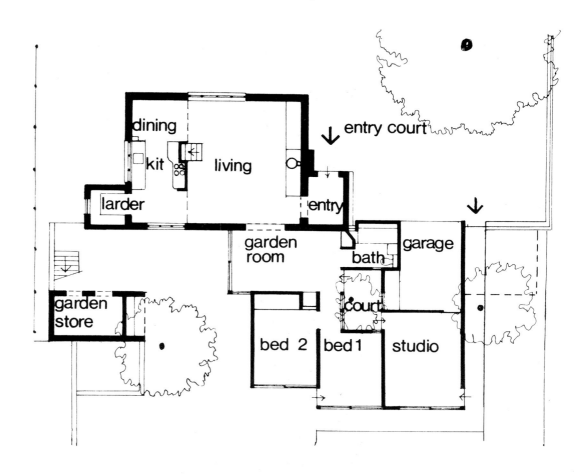

73 — View of living room towards
first floor deck. Dining at right,
kitchen is behind stairs.

74 — The sleeping deck

75 — An angled view towards
first floor deck; note the
two-level gallery

half of the existing two-storey brick shell is
now a full height living area. Opposite, a timber
two-level gallery has many uses: it provides a
suspended ceiling over the more intimate
dining area, gives access to the upper level,
and acts as space divider separating the
kitchen, placed behind the stairs, from the
living area.

On the upper level there are a sleeping deck,
dressing and bathrooms. Furniture is mostly
built-in. An intelligent use of space and a
sensitive and direct manner of handling timber
are in fact the most important factors for the
success of this conversion.

76 – The studio, in the new wing
77 – The central court

78 – The back elevation as seen from the old garden

The single storey extension is of large ship-lap boarding on a timber frame, finished with timber boarding and plaster board. The block is connected to the house by a garden room, a partially enclosed space leading to a cluster of two bedrooms, studio, garage and bathroom. In planning the new wing great care was taken to preserve all trees in the area, and this controlled dimensions and design to some extent. One result of this concept is a central courtyard, formed around an existing tree, that catches the sun and provides extra daylight to the new rooms.

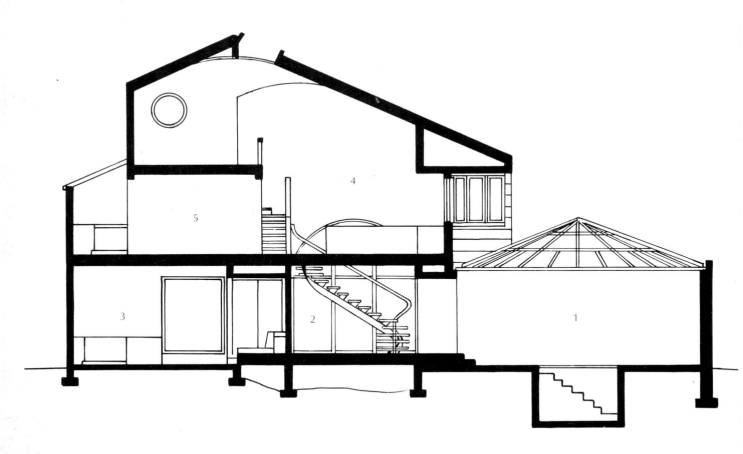

79 – Sectional plan

1 Enclosed pool
2 Gallery
3 Study
4 Bedroom
5 Bathroom

An Extension to a Modern House in Tacoma, Washington

An extension to an earlier residence was needed to provide a new master bedroom suite, space for an extensive art collection, and an enclosed small pool for therapy and recreation. Two round brick patios, designed by the same architect for a previous addition, inspired the curvilinear forms, adopted in open contrast with the main structure.

The access is from the smaller patio to the round brick pavilion surmounted by a glass and metal skylight, a solution that will be repeated throughout to ensure privacy and light. In the centre of the blue tiled floor is the pool. A

double door leads to the gallery, a space connecting the extension to the main house, with a door to the study and stairs to the upper level. The floor is of the same blue tiles used for the pool; a colour repeated, together with shades of green and yellow fading towards the top, on the handsome stained glass window by Steve Shahbaghlian. Lighting is by movable spotlights on parallel tracks.

The wooden stairs sweep directly into the master bedroom and to a small gallery above. On this level wood is used extensively to frame the precise architectural details, and to

80 – The enclosed pool, used for therapy and leisure

81 – Entrance to the extension from enclosed pool

82 – The powder room area at the end of dressing area

83 – Looking from bedroom to dressing area: the small gallery is used as a tiny study

Overpage

84 – Detail of gallery showing part of the stained glass window

line the curving ceiling. One end of the bedroom is shaped as an inverted bay and looks onto the garden, just above the glass dome of the pool. The other end leads through a dressing area to a semicircular powder room, lined with mirrors and completely surmounted by a large skylight.

Architect: Stephen Yakeley
Interior Designer: Mrs B Smith

Photography by Richard Einzig

A Family House near Cambridge, England

85 – Outside view of the south elevation. The entrance is to the right; at the extreme left side of the building are french doors to open plan-living/dining

This house for a distinguished metallurgist, his artist wife and their two children, had to satisfy some rather special requirements. The living, dining and kitchen areas were to be an open space overlooked by a studio on the first floor; a large garage for a collection of vintage cars and a display area for the wife's paintings and sculptures were also needed.

The architect had known Dr and Mrs Smith for some years, and shared with Mrs Smith a remarkable similarity of attitudes to architecture. This meant that very few

alterations were made to the original plan, and also that Mrs Smith's interior design did in effect relate to the entire building.

The main shape is of two slightly asymmetrical wings separated by a skylit stair. The larger wing has the garage and the open living area overlooked by the studio; the other is a sleeping area, with playroom and store on the first floor. The service tower at the rear of the house contains chimney flues, electrical equipment, plumbing vents and watertanks; a minor alteration made to the original design

86 – Floor plans

87 – Sectional plans

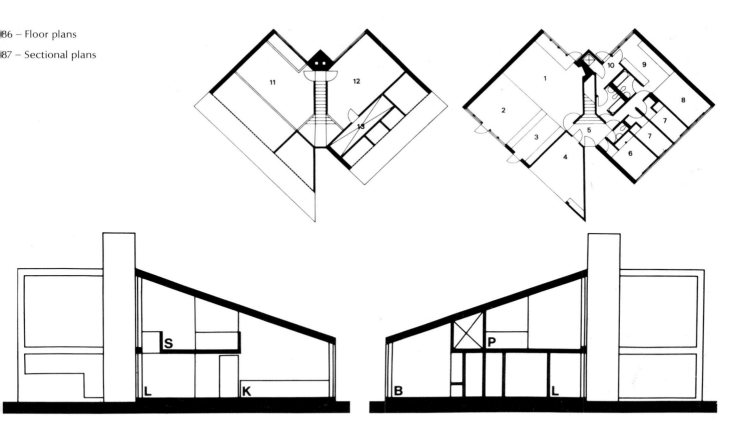

88 – View of reception area
from garden

89 – Dining/kitchen area; the studio is at left above

90 – The living area, under the studio

was to abolish the sharp angle of the tower and insert a window, so that one could enjoy a view of the fields to the north while climbing the stairway.

On mass concrete foundations, the cavity walls are externally of brown facing bricks with grey mortar; the interior 'skin' is a sandwich of facing brick and thermal insulating block. The roof slopes up to provide space for the first floor studio and playroom; it has brown concrete tiles on timber joists. Window and door frames are black stained timber both outside and inside.

Brown, grey, black, tan are also the colours of the interior, balanced by large areas of white on the flat ceilings and on some walls and furniture. The restrained range of colour is enhanced by a variety of textures that in the living space contraposes velvet to exposed brick. A glass and steel low table rests on a deep pile rug, carpet adjoins floor tiles, white plaster sharply defines the sloping ceilings of western red cedar boarding. In a final synthesis of colour, the handsome abstract painting in the living corner appears to belong naturally to the wall on which it is displayed. The total effect is subtle and harmonious.

91 – View of master bedroom from dressing room

92 – Main entrance; stairs lead to studio, left, and playroom, right. Bedroom wing is at right; living to the left

93 – View over the fields from studio

94 – The house as seen from the fields to the north

95 – Ground plan

1 Entrance
2 Kitchen
3 Bathroom
4 Studio/office

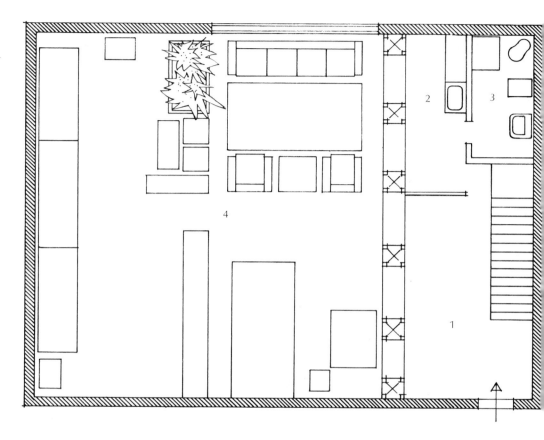

Studio for a Stage Designer in Rome, Italy

96 – The steel structure; to the left, the mirror on the kitchen partition reflects the entrance door

The pleasing proportions of this century-old building allowed ample freedom of scope to an imaginative architect such as Pier Luigi Pizzi, who is also a stage designer. Located in that extraordinary area of Rome included between Piazza del Popolo and via del Babuino, this 8m × 10m × 8m cube was, a century ago, a studio for a sculptor and ceramist; then it was used as a ballet school. When the present owner found it he felt that his painstaking search for a studio of his own had come to an end. He was yet to enjoy an added bonus when the demolition of a badly damaged ceiling revealed the original roof beams and a very valuable skylight. This discovery gave Pizzi the idea of juxtaposing a stainless steel

grid, the shape that expresses so well much of the architecture of our time, to the splendid 19th century exposed wooden beams. Once this starting point was decided, the entire solution came as if of its own accord.

A steel structure, occupying one third of the whole width of the floor space, incorporates entrance hall, small kitchen, bathroom, and stairs leading to a rest area 3.50m above ground. A mirror covering the kitchen partition reflects the pattern of the grid, and adds both interest and visual depth. The remaining area is left open, with furniture arranged so as to define different areas of use. A writing table, drawing board and a large

97 – Conversation and storage area as seen from the rest area above

98 – Study area as seen from conversation area

Overpage

99 – An overall view of the studio from the rest area

painting, 'Oedipus Rex' by Lorenzo Tornabuoni, for the study. The conversation area has simple, unassuming armchair units, but on a glass and steel table rest a head of Parian marble (Greek art of 1st century BC) and a Roman copy of a Greek torso (1st century AD). On the wall facing the steel grid there is another painting, by Mario Schifano. Steel and glass bookshelves and a trough of green plants partly hide the longe range of fitted filing cabinets. White paint on the walls and the original terracotta tiles on the floor harmonize with the colour and texture of the roof beams, emphasizing the simple elegance of this outstanding conversion.

The Official Residence for the Prefect of the Essonne, France

100 – Entrance hall; facing the door is the brick mural by Thomas Gleb

101 – Detail of mural

The formal reception wing in the residence of one of France's chief civil administrators is L-shaped, with walls mainly of glass supported by slender concrete pillars. The basic structure demanded an open plan arrangement for the interior, with minimal brickwork to define private areas. A subtle interplay of different textures was essential to the scheme, to counteract both 'hard edge' materials such as glass, concrete, highly polished white marble, and the bleaching effect of stark daylight.

The designer kept the brickwork in evidence, but painted it white to exclude any 'rustic' undertones, which in this case would be

totally out of place. Just in front of the entrance, an integrated mural by Thomas Gleb exploits the pattern of brickwork and gives movement to the inner wall. The main reception is sub-divided by two large swivelling doors separating dining from conversation area. The dining room is dominated by the table, composed of square units of stainless steel which can be added to each other to accommodate up to 32 guests. The formal severity of this space is tempered by a large, thick white carpet and by the long and narrow trough containing a miniature indoor garden.

In the entertainment area light is controlled

102 – Looking from conversation
to dining area; the two spaces
can be completely separated by
two swivelling doors

by white curtains of Tergal and raw silk, which
cover the entire glass walls, and by numerous
dimmer-controlled lights set above the
suspended ceiling of blonde Oregon pine. Here
again, thick white carpets contrast with
polished marble floor and with the steel and
plate glass circular nests of tables. The only
colour in the furnishing is given by the brandy-
coloured leather covering sofas and armchairs.
At the extreme end of the room, flanked by
two long seats of natural leather, is the
stainless steel open fireplace designed by the
sculptor Philolaos. Its graceful convoluted
form epitomizes the character of the whole
scheme: direct, simple, yet supremely elegant.

103 – The modular dinner table,
a design by Pierre Guariche

104 – Overall view of the
conversation space; the glass
and steel nest of tables is by the
designer, Pierre Guariche. In the
background can be seen the
fireplace by Philolaos

Architect: Alan Liddle

Photography by Richard Rubicam and
Chas. R Pearson

The Residence of the Architect in Tacoma, Washington

The plan of this residence had to be flexible enough to provide for the entertainment of large groups and for the needs of particular family patterns, with a minimum of maintenance of house and garden.

Surrounded by heavy woods, the house looks onto a quiet lake. The climate is generally cool, so there was the desire to catch as much sun as possible and to shelter the house from the cold north winds blowing from the lake. By placing the carport on the approach side, and linking this to the main house with a

long cloister the architect created an inner court that acts as a sun trap. All roofs slope at different angles to assist reflection of sunlight and add architectural interest. Above the carpo is a tiny apartment which can be used as a second bedroom and bath.

Access to the house is under a low trellis to the right, through iron gates into the cloister, and into the small entrance hall that has an 18 ft high ceiling. This room leads to a large open space, where day and night areas merge both on the horizontal and the vertical plane.

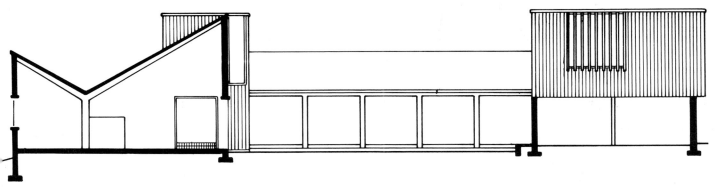

105 – Approach; to the right a
ow trellis leads to the cloister

106 – Plans
  1 Carport
  2 Portico
  3 Cloister
  4 Court
  5 Pool
  6 Entrance
  7 Living/dining/kitchen
  8 Back entrance
  9 Bedroom
 10 Bathroom
 11 Utility

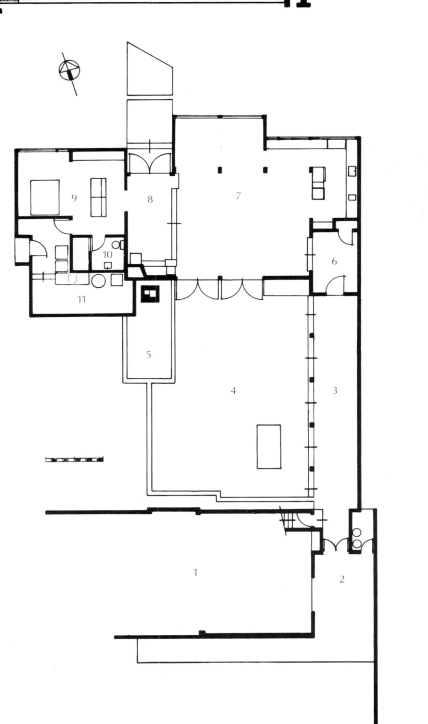

Overpage

107 – Detail of living area, with
doors opening to the forest side.
Through the doorway, beyond
the bookcase that doubles as
wardrobe on the other side, is
the bedroom

108 – Detail of living area; large
glass doors to inner court. The
light fixtures are cubes of
Plexiglas with a prismatic
texture hung under a two-foot
square skylight. On left background is the kitchen

109 – Living and dining area as seen from entrance hall

110 – Detail of bedroom

111 – View from the inner court,
showing water spouting from the
tall chimney

Dining, kitchen, living areas flow into each
other; the ceiling opens into skylights, sunlight
pours in from many directions. Even artificial
lighting seems to emphasize the absence of a
distinct separation between day and night, as
three 'day-light fixtures' also incorporate
electric lights for night-time illumination.
Definition of function is however present
through ingenious and witty details, such as
the bright posters lining a kitchen cupboard
on the dining side, or the wardrobe in the
bedroom which doubles as bookcase on the

side facing the living area. The entire house is
essentially one large space with doors only to
utility and bath rooms.

Materials are simple: wood, white paint for
ceiling and walls; the same brick tiles are used
inside and outside. Large double glass doors
open onto the court; a pool reflects the
surrounding dense forest, left in its natural
state; water spouts from near the top of the
tall brick chimney sitting within the pool – a
supremely witty example of duality of function.

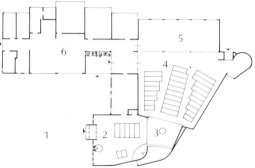

The Church of St Joseph in Geilenkirchen-Bauchem, West Germany

An initial plan for a church intended to serve the combined parishes of Geilenkirchen-Bauchem and Geilenkirchen-Niederheid was developed into that for a small community centre after the appointment of the present parish priest, whose ideas were strongly in favour of a more socially oriented function of the Church. The architect was then given a new brief, more challenging both from the architectural and the financial point of view, since no additional resources would be made available to cover the cost of an increased number of buildings.

To ensure the success of the project, a long and detailed consultation took place between the architect and the stained glass artist

Ludwig Schaffrath. The two men had been associated over a long period of time, and shared the same belief in the integration of architecture and the art of contemporary stained glass. Opposing the idea of commissioning 'a stained glass window' once the building process was well under way, the design of this church includes structures of precast concrete, as well as glass, lead, light, colour, as means to artistic expression. The same concept is carried out inside, where concrete pillars placed immediately in front of the main window define protectively the baptismal area and direct light on the important elements associated with religious rituals: font, tabernacle, altar, standing cross and ceremoni chandeliers. Also designed by Ludwig Schaffrat

these pieces are cast in bronze or carved out of blocks of Belgian granite.

The plan of the church is articulated into three distinct units: a plain copper door leads to a small church , seating about 35 people and used for weekday service, prayers and the reservation of the Sacrament; a large, elbow-shaped raised platform, with the tabernacle at its right lower end and the circular altar placed off centre; and finally an apron-shaped larger church room for 250 people, used both for Sunday service, in combination with the small church, and for concerts. A rectangular annex at the back of the church is for conferences, film shows and other secular activities, or can be added to the church by opening a sliding partition. Three additional common rooms are for teaching and club activitie

The materials are very simple: the load-bearing walls are brick sandwiched between precast concrete slabs, for the outside, and insulating block faced with finely ribbed Hochloch-Poroton tiles for the interior. The ceiling over the altar is spruce boarding. Over the seating areas are suspended acoustic ceiling structures of moulded plaster painted red, that also contain concealed light fixtures. The floor and platforms are black artificial stone inlaid with green marble. Benches, doors and organ loft are pine.

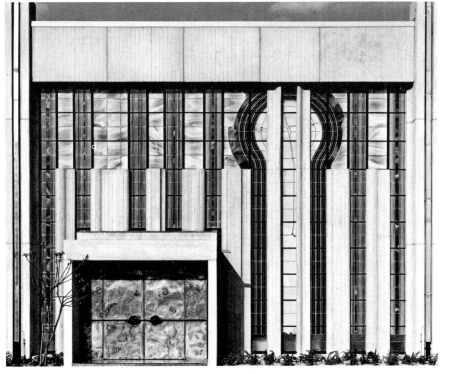

115 – View of the small church;
in the background is the circular
altar

116 – View from the larger church

117 – Detail of outside structure,
showing the perfect integration
between concrete pillars and
stained glass windows

But an arid description of details cannot
convey the feeling of intense spiritual fervour
that is expressed by the stained windows. They
occupy almost the entire facade; opal and
antique clear glass went into their construction;
and an outstanding feature of their design,
characteristic of Ludwig Schaffrath's art, is that
the lead, employed in the past merely as a
connecting medium between the sections of
glass, is used here as an integral part of the
aesthetic concept.

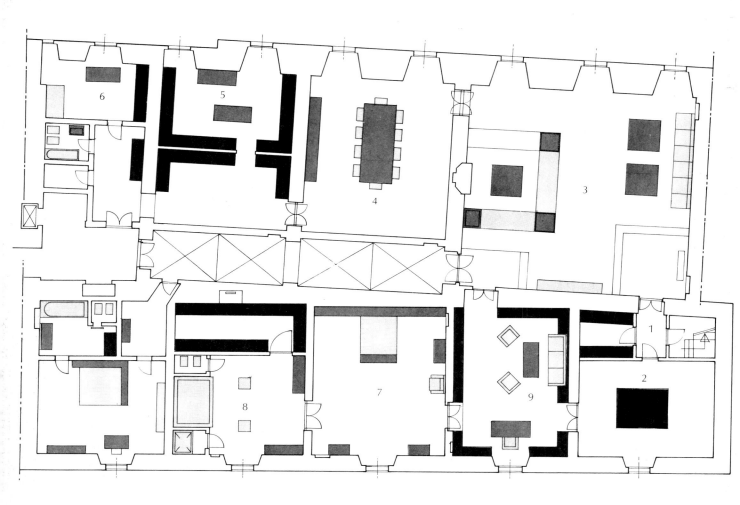

An Apartment for a Collector of Modern Art in Rome, Italy

119 – The entrance gallery; on left foreground a Perspex sculpture, on the right a painting by Canaletto, in the background a sculpture by Trouva. Through the open door can be seen the reception room

The apartment occupies a wing of a 17th century palace, an important example of Roman Baroque architecture. This fact alone would tax the proven ability of any architect called upon to create an environment that would express trends, inclinations, the life of our times without losing sight of the grandiose scale of the Baroque setting. In this case the apartment is also the home of one of the most impressive collections of American modern art to be found in Europe. Nearly all contemporary artists are represented: works by Stella, Warhol, Wesselmann, Motherwell, Dine, are in every

room; they become part of the life of the house.

Whether the original architecture was left intact, as in the magnificent entrance hall, or whether spaces have been moulded into modern proportions by changes in floor levels, use of partitions, or by suspended ceilings, one is always aware of a breadth of vision that communicates to a seemingly unemotional interaction of architectural volumes a powerful, majestic rhythm. This is due to a felicitous combination of an infallible perception of space, an acute sensitivity to new materials

120 – The dining room; on the back wall a painting by Frank Stella, to the right a piece by Vasarely and to the left a 1963 painting by Tom Wesselmann. The dining table is a design by Beverly Pepper

Overpage

121 – The reception room as seen from the conversation pit. In the background, a painting by Robert Motherwell is flanked by two 18th century Venetian sculptures. To the right, a piece by Louise Nevelson

and colours and, above all, to a passionate
love for art.

Walls and ceilings are white and glossy,
reflections blur the boundaries of walls,
reduced in size to harmonize with the scale
of modern art pieces. The subtle arrangement
of light is intended to create the exact
atmosphere, never to project a crude spotlight
on a particular painting or sculpture. A
uniform, sand-coloured carpet covers reception
and dining room floors – a subdued, soft
texture contrasting with the polychromatic

marbles of the palatial hall. The doors between
these rooms are by Jean Claude Fahi; made
of brown Perspex with a sculpted motif of
multilayered iridescent lamination, they seem
to gather all the colours of the rainbow, and
are works of art in their own right. The dining
table of brown lacquer rests on an iron base
designed by Beverly Pepper, the dining armchairs of brown suède and lacquered metal
were especially designed by the architects.
In this room striking multicolour light effects
are produced by luminous bands running
along floor and ceiling.

122 – The master bedroom

123 – The bathroom

The master bedroom is in various tonalities of brown, with light touches of white and yellow. On the walls, 'Mouth with Cigarette' by Tom Wesselmann and 'Red Cut' by Fontana. Adjacent to the bedroom is a vast bathroom of basaltic stone and steel. On the slate grey background, accents of vivid crimson and gold suggest an atmosphere of sumptuousness; unexpectedly in such surroundings, a Louis XV armchair with petit-point tapestry faces a piece by Michelangelo Pistoletto, 'Trompe l'Oeil'.

A Church and Community Centre
for Oulunkylä, Finland

125 – Outside view of main church

The concept of a community centre where the traditional functions of the church could be combined with additional social activities, offered by the church, has been predominant in church building techniques of recent years. The Oulunkylä Church is the first example in the history of Finnish architecture where the idea of a multipurpose church has been worked out thoroughly. Client, architects, and a team of artists devised a plan that defined in detail all functional and aesthetic elements, from the architectural frame to the design of interior fittings, ceremonial dressing and silver implements.

The main concept was to maintain a solemnity to the prime function of the building – that of a church – and then allow a plurality of uses within the space. Apart from the main church and a small chapel for wedding and other ceremonies, there had to be administrative offices, youth and adult club rooms, and a kindergarten.

The structure, on two levels, is a reinforced concrete frame filled in with dark red bricks. The outside is a closed shell of brickwork, only interrupted by the entrance door and by a large window on the upper level. Inside, the

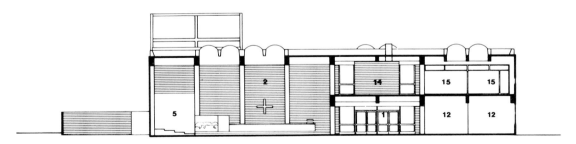

126 – Sectional plan

127 – Main church as seen from
the entrance; the organ was
designed by Matti Rindell and
built by Kangasalan Urkutehdas

128 – Another view of the church

129 – Detail of altar and chair. The red pine sculpture is by Raimo Heino

concrete pillars and roof beams are exposed and painted white; together with the red brick walls and glass skylights they form a grid of natural materials that with its colours and textures provides the appropriate setting for the art pieces. A visual link between the various parts of the building is obtained by using glass for the inner walls of the club rooms on the second floor. On important occasions this space can function as a gallery to the main church. The ground floor is also articulated by movable partitions that create areas for private meetings. The seating is also movable.

130 – Detail of upper hall; the
sculpture by Marjatta
Weckström is of light concrete

131 – Outside view with bell
tower

Daylight is admitted through large glass
squares in the roof; light boxes are placed
in clusters of four at the intersections of the
ceiling beams. The main interior fittings are
permanent; the altar, chair and christening
font are all of red brick. The altar railing is of
dark painted metal, the chairs are covered of
blue fabric. Floors are dark red tiles throughout.

Architects: Giancarlo and Luigi Bicocchi, Roberto Monsani

Photography by Carla de Benedetti

A Conversion near Florence, Italy

132 – Outside view of portico and garden; the house is to the left

133 – Detail of the living room

134 – Plan

1 Entrance
2 Dining
3 Kitchen
4 Study
5 Living

Restoration was the most delicate and sensitive stage during the conversion of this house, placed on one of the hills surrounding Florence. The history of the original building is somewhat incomplete: it is known that it was a convent of considerable antiquity and that towards the end of the 19th century it was converted into several private dwellings. The subject of this feature is one of these.

The house has a view over a large garden adjoining a 19th century portico, built as a free interpretation of an older portico represented in a fresco found within the existing structure.

On the ground floor are the entrance hall, living room, study and dining room, all with doors to the portico. The bedrooms and a large terrace are on the floor above. Since the building was listed, there was no possibility of adding substantial masonry work; so the architects concentrated on emphasizing the serene, almost monastic atmosphere of the place, expressing a precise desire to restore the original structure so far as possible.

The furnishing plays a very important part in the success of this project, unifying all spaces with the simplicity of white paint and coarse

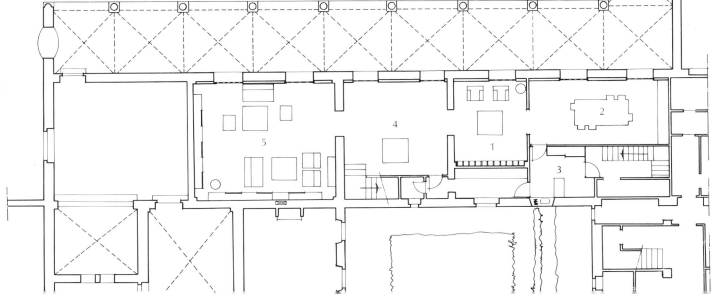

135 – Entrance hall, with a
roundel by Jacopo del Sellaio

136 – Overall view of the living
room

sisal matting; sliding doors of brown laminate
are repeated rhythmically throughout the
ground floor; large low tables, and movable
spotlights contribute to the unobtrusive,
measured elegance of the scheme. The owner's
love for old masters is expressed by a landscape
by Salvator Rosa, in the dining room, and by a
roundel by Jacopo del Sellaio in the entrance,
that reminds one of the frescoes by the school
of Giotto covering the walls of the private
chapel contiguous to the house (not shown
here). The living room occupies probably the
convent chapter, or meeting, room. The very
high ribbed vault has been left intact, but to

reduce the space to a more intimate scale a
continuous panel of square modules runs along
three main walls. A special indirect lighting effect
is obtained by exploring a chessboard pattern
with alternate light and dark elements. The
square motif is repeated in different proportions
in the design of the large doors opening onto the
portico. Armchairs and sofas are very low, as if to
suggest a continuous horizontal level. Designed
by the architects, they are suède cushions
contained within a shell of Perspex.

137 – Dining room; the table is a design by the architects; on the back wall, a painting by Salvator Rosa

138 – The portico and garden as seen from the entrance hall

Architect: Arata Isozaki   Photography by Osamu Murai and
                                            Kuniharu Sakumoto

139 – General view across the
lawn from the Monroe Gate,
whose shape is a symbolic
celebration of the actress
Marilyn Monroe

The Gumma Prefectural Museum
of Modern Art in Takasaki, Japan

Arata Isozaki described the Gumma Prefectural Museum of Modern Art as 'cubic frames placed beyond a flat lawn as if they were thrown at random'. And this is exactly what the basic structure appears to be. But one must proceed further. The shadows cast by the cubic frames suggest the infinite aesthetic possibilities afforded by inserting more cubes of the same size into the existing ones, and symbolize the principle governing the expanding space. 'Cubic form is not only simple and clear,' continues Arata Isozaki, 'but is also the ultimate in terms of three-dimensional space, an absolute

form. It is coherent with the rigid-joint steel frame structure which supports from within the entire heritage of modern architecture since Louis Sullivan's time. Like the Greek order, the Roman arch, and the dome of the Renaissance, it is closely related to the style of the times with its proven universality. As an ornament, in this sense, the cubic frames adopted in the plan of this Museum emphasize its monumentality.

However, the nature of a Museum of Modern Art must need be ambivalent. One of its sections is used for the exhibition of the

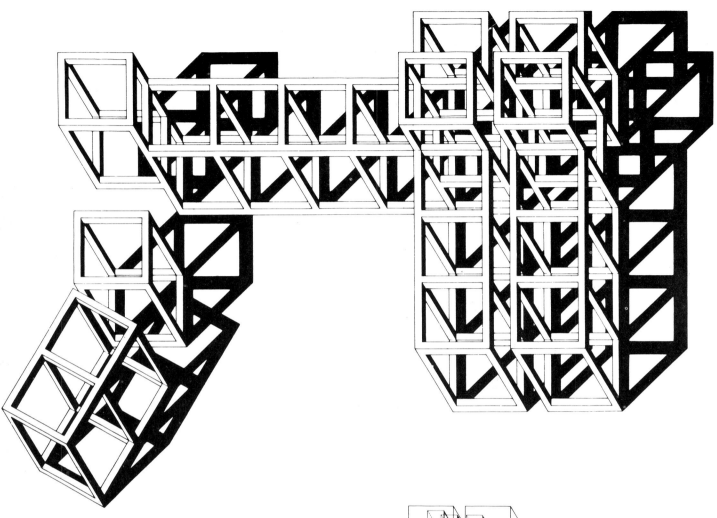

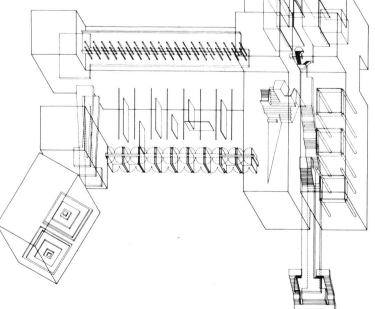

140 – Basic structure

141 – Supplemental structure

142 – Main entrance hall as seen from stairs to upper gallery

permanent modern art collection, the other is only a temporary abode for works of art which, with frames and pedestals, are moving throughout the world. In the first instance it is possible to design the exhibition hall according to its contents. One can create areas of darkness with artificial lighting, or the skylight can be used to dramatize impact. But a space meant to exhibit ever changing, unpredictable collections of objects, should be as neutral as possible. Ideally, walls and ceilings should become an even source of indirect light; then the shadows from every exhibit would disappear,

and with them all feeling of material weight would go. The visitor would behold the work of art alone.

To pursue this ideal Arata Isozaki reacted against the rigidity of the adopted modular cubic structure. He used a floor surface that is flat and smooth and extends to the front lawn, where open air exhibitions are held: boundaries begin to merge. A thin film of translucent material lines walls and ceilings, mirrors surfaces and outside trees in the entrance hall. Indirect lighting blurs edges.

143 – View of stairs from main
entrance

Significantly, the section containing the
permanent exhibition is projected diagonally,
at an angle of 22.5°, over the pond. Its reversed
image, distorted by the movement of the water,
becomes ambiguous. Unexpected relationships
develop.

144 – An angled view of main staircase showing the effect of reflection on highly polished surfaces

145 – An exhibition hall; note how the concept of the cubic module is carried throughout, to include display boxes and pedestals

146 – Outside display area projecting over the pond (to the right); reflections of the water on the ceiling

147 – Another view of the open
air exhibition area looking
towards main gate across the
pond

148 – Looking from the pond to
main entrance hall, reflected on
the glass and polished stone of
the facade

The Art of Fibre
by Virginia West

The art of fibre is the single most vigorous movement in the art world today. Interest in ethnical history and in ancient art has attracted weavers to the far regions of Latin America, India, Africa, where they have often participated in the activities of small communities whose livelihood depends on textile crafts. Relics of ceremonial garments found in the tombs of ancient cities have been studied with reverence, traditional processes and techniques invested with poetic meaning, and in so doing artists have rediscovered their medium. This movement has reverberated throughout the world of contemporary art, and now has painters trying to capture the tactile, textural qualities of fibres; who shred or tear their canvases to effect the changeable surface planes of weaving. And sculptors, turning from rigid, inflexible materials have abandoned steel for the flowing properties of fibre.

Weaving arose from the fundamental need to protect man from the elements and evolved in all cultures in response to materials available. The weaver enjoyed a special status in tribal life; he was part of a sacred cult where mystery and magic became associated with the weaving process. The objects of beauty produced were thought to be inspired by divine motivation, and the weaver was accorded privileges second only to those of priests. Remnants that have survived in the arid desert sands of Peru, the peat bogs of Denmark, the Chinese burial mounds, give testimony to acts of faith outlasting the civilizations that produced them.

'Masterpieces of Tapestry', from the 14th to 16th centuries, shown at the Grand Palais in Paris in 1973 and again at the New York's Metropolitan, was an awe-inspiring exhibition. These tapestries recalled a time when kings competed for the limited output of the ateliers at Brussels, Bruges and Tournai, and then flaunted their acquisitions as symbols of wealth and power. Used functionally to absorb the dankness of the castle interior, tapestry at the same time surfaced the walls with a splendour of pictorial narrative that visually blotted the walls from memory. The church used tapestry as an apocalyptic warning to those who pursued evil. One such series still exists at Angers, miraculously rescued from the floors of stables following the Revolution.

The physical act of weaving a tapestry required prodigious efforts on the part of many people, and a division of responsibility had to be made. Reluctant to trust the cartoons to the corps of weavers, artists of the calibre of Rubens and Raphäel would provide drawings, which were numbered and then followed slavishly by workers whose names were omitted in archival accounts. There are signs that weavers strongly resented this lack of confidence and that they were eventually granted the right to design small background areas. Fortunately, this tradition has reversed itself. Today's textile artist is involved in the process of weaving from conception to realization, and he often performs all aspects of the work himself. However, there is still a tendency, which seems archaic in the context of modern fibre art, to copy in tapestry paintings by artists such as Léger, Calder and Le Corbusier. Had Le Corbusier ever worked at the loom, had he ever manipulated fibre, he would have focused his creative genius on the structural and textural possibilities inherent in fibre, rather than impose on it the disciplines of a far different medium.

The current robust activity springs from many sources and is a profound breakthrough. International exhibitions no longer separate fibre from the 'fine' arts of painting and sculpture. The São Paulo Biennial awarded weaver Magdalena Abakanowicz of Poland a gold medal on the basis of her art, not her medium; the Venice Biennial and the Milan Triennial have welcomed the fibre art of Swiss Elsi Giauque, German Ritzi and Peter Jacobi, Italian Sandra Marconato, Argentine Maria Simon, and others. In 1969 three major shows in three countries, 'Perspectief in Textiel' at the Stedelijk in Amsterdam, 'Wall Hangings' at the

Museum of Modern Art in New York, and 'Experienças Artisticas Textiles' at the Museo de Arte Contemporáneo in Madrid, presented to a stunned public the new art forms in fibre. No longer confined to rectilinear parameters or to two-dimensional planar surfaces, shaped, pendulous, often free-standing structures caused museum officials and art critics alike to sit up and take notice. 'Deliberate Entanglements' at the University of California Art Galleries in Los Angeles in 1971 gave still more impetus to the surge of fibre expression. Altogether seven 'Biennales Internationales de la Tapisserie' in Lausanne have recorded the revolutionary change in fibre as an art idiom. The Swiss biennials imposed a five square metre minimum size limit; the British Crafts Centre countered the preoccupation with overwhelming scale with an international exhibition in London, in 1974, called 'Miniature Textiles', where the limit was up to 20 cm (8 inches) in any direction. Aurelia Muñoz (Spain) demonstrated that a 20 cm Plexiglas cube could spawn the structure, and be a containment, for a knotted form. Sheila Hicks (United States) wove letter-size compressed memories in fibre, intensely personal. Olga de Amaral (Columbia) stacked woven fragments vertically, applied gesso to edges and displayed these collages that possess the delicacy and grace of miniature carved ivories. Wilhelmina Fruytier (The Netherlands) translated heroic architectural constructions into reduced size, and they worked equally well. Her 'Moon Trip' in white cotton is illustrated. Herman Scholten (The Netherlands) and Moik Schiele (Switzerland) also transferred to small scale large pieces of work with no lessening of impact. Archie Brennan (England) wove genre objects, a fried egg, a package complete with postage stamp, tapestry tours de force. His command of the medium is illustrated by 'Corner Piece'. 'Danish Expressions in Textiles', which opened in Copenhagen in August 1975, is touring United States galleries under the auspices of the Smithsonian Institution. The show is characterized by the timeless understated simplicity of Vibeke Klint, the hard edge geometric tapestries of Jette Thyssen, the prismatic, mosaic-like compositions of Berit Hjelholt, the large dynamic series tapestries of Kim Naver. All exemplify scrupulous craftsmanship and reflect the ascetic temperance of the Danes, which rejects extremes of fad and non-functionalism. 'Textile Objekte' began in Berlin at the Kunstgewerbemuseum and toured Germany until August 1976, presenting fibre objects by

thirty-six invited artists of international renown. The newest trend emerging from 'Textile Objekte' is the flat manipulated fibre plane, evidenced in the exciting tent-form by Susanne Hepfinger (Germany). Her 'Kultisches Zelt' derives from ethnic sources, deep in folk art tradition; displayed as an A-frame, its surface is broken by colourful geometric distribution. Stronger than ever is the work of Peter and Ritzi Jacobi, a husband-wife duo, born in Rumania, now living and working in Germany. 'Exotica', a series of tapestries, indicates a new direction for this talented couple. Hundreds of small sisal cylinders, wrapped with wool, cotton and raw silk, break from the surface in organic, growth-like profusion, defying gravity in their upright orientation. The effect is of constant, kinetic movement.

The prestigious 1975 'Biennale Internationale de la Tapisserie' in Lausanne, Switzerland, attracted 765 dossiers from 64 countries. The stated objective of the competition is to chart developing trends worldwide. And there are many! Although there were a few decorative, two-dimensional works that employed traditional tapestry technique, the more exciting were those with an innovative twist. Judit Droppa, from Hungary, wove strips that formed mitered flaps on the vertical surface; Sandra Marconato, from Italy, used continuous loop finials that defied explanation. Polish Janina Tworek-Pierzgalska created an environmental room, called 'Places', with its special precincts for sitting, lying, standing, kneeling. However, the most sensational were the startling extensions of the use of fibre as artistic expression.

The contemporary weaver no longer relies solely on familiar organic fibres such as wool, linen, cotton and silk; he is likely to try copper tubing, sausage casing, vinyl film, wire, epoxies, leather, polypropylene ropes, foam rubber. The loom has to be mastered, but it is only one of the ways to interlace threads: a simple frame may impose fewer restrictions. Grau-Garriga, from Spain, employs the most primitive of frames, sans heddles, from which issue complex multi-layered hangings. Uninhibited rope wefts and unconstrained clumps of yarn hang freely, defy containment by architectural space. Trained in the tight tapestry technique of Aubusson, it is as though, having mastered his lessons, he revolted to forge his own way, and in so doing broke all rules. His attitude is that he is an artist first, and weaving is his language. The ancient art of knotting requires

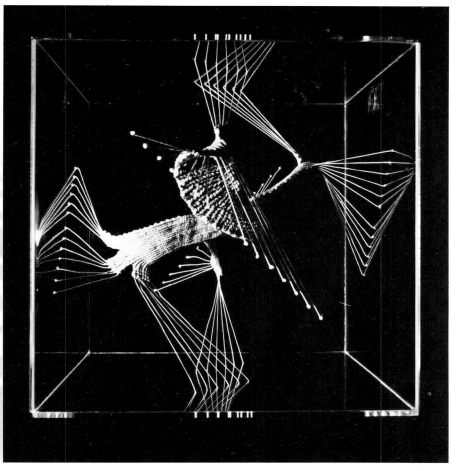

152 – 'Le Bassin. Triptychon II';
Linen thread, embroidery
techniques; 20 × 8 ($8\frac{7}{8}$ × $3\frac{1}{8}$)
Made by Liselotte Siegfried,
Switzerland

153 – 'Concha abierta'; the
controlled flare and textural
effect is obtained by adding
strands of yarn to execute the
different bands; knotting
technique, white linen;
54 × 25 × 23 ($21\frac{1}{4}$ × $9\frac{7}{8}$ × $11\frac{3}{4}$)
Made by Aurelia Muñoz, Spain

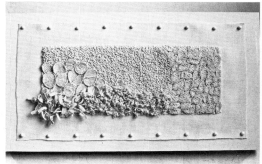

150 – 'Concha', a knotted spiral
anchored within a box of
Perspex; white linen 22 × 22
($8\frac{5}{8}$ × $8\frac{5}{8}$)
Made by Aurelia Muñoz, Spain

151 – 'Souvenir Insaisissable I';
dark indigo form, expressing
poetical associations with
natural dyes and the symbolism
of colours; cotton material
stuffed and tied with webbing;
20 × 10 × 10 ($7\frac{7}{8}$ × 4 × 4)
Made by Daniel Graffin, France

156 – 'Fragmento completo';
natural linen wrapped with rust
and gold, blue fibres, touched
with gesso; 30 × 15 (11¾ × 5⅞)
Made by Olga de Amaral,
Colombia

154 – 'Himmel'; the luminous
quality of this piece is obtained
by the hanging silken wefts,
coloured in tones from dark blue
to aquamarine; 17 × 20 × 20
(7⅞ × 6¾ × 6¾)
Made by Moik Schiele,
Switzerland

155 – 'Looped stitch'; raw wool,
spot wrapped, and blue cotton
lace; 15 × 16 (6¼ × 5⅞)
Made by Claire Zeisler, USA

no equipment at all, save for the hoists and
pulleys to suspend rope structures. Françoise
Grossen, (United States) whose 'Five Rivers' is
illustrated, braids manila rope, dyed in tones of
blue and purple, with economy of means and
of statement. The composition recalls the ebb
and flow of the tributaries of a river. Macramé,
originally a decorative knotting method of
finishing the fringe ends of a weaving off the
loom, is the basis of Aurelia Muñoz's art.
Basketry, once a loving pursuit of almost every

tribe, in danger of becoming extinct, has been
revived by scholarly investigation and
simultaneous adaptation of long-forgotten
techniques. Gary Trentham (United States)
practises the basket-making technique of old
using contemporary materials and produces
a modern objet d'art.

Those who do use the loom have attained
tremendous self-discipline and superb technica
mastery. These weavers are in the minority.

157 – 'Family of threads' weaving technique; linen, wool and synthetic fibres; 20 × 16 ($7\frac{7}{8}$ × $6\frac{1}{4}$)
Made by Desirée Scholten de Rivière, Holland

158 – 'Enroulements'; separate bands of woven goat hair are rolled and sewn down; 13 × 18 × 5 ($5\frac{1}{8}$ × 7 × 2)
Made by Cyril Bourquin-Walfard, Switzerland

159 – 'Drawn paper texture'; woven paper, dyed and drawn; 18 × 13 (7 × $5\frac{1}{8}$)
Made by Herman Scholten, Holland

A lifetime is necessary to discover the possibilities the loom affords : shaping, layering, three-dimensional structuring, volumetric cascading – the repertoire can only expand as knowledge increases. Trude Guermonprez, professor at California College of Arts and Crafts, typifies this philosophy. Her approach is intellectual, developing out of confident understanding. 'Images II' uses one of the basic principles of weaving, weft flats, on a simple ribbed background, as the linear element of design. The piece is turned 90° from the way in which it was woven but works in any direction. Elsi Giauque of Switzerland can make the loom perform miracles: 'Trinity, the Five Phantoms', is a five-part, multi-level loom-executed weaving. It is suspended vertically to separate levels and unwoven groups of warp threads encircled in colour, in a controlled optical pattern.

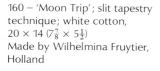

160 – 'Moon Trip'; slit tapestry
technique; white cotton,
20 × 14 ($7\frac{7}{8}$ × $5\frac{1}{2}$)
Made by Wilhelmina Fruytier,
Holland

161 – 'Serie A No. 11'; hand
sewing technique, white linen;
12 × 7.5 ($4\frac{3}{4}$ × 3)
Made by Corrie de Boer, Holland

162 – 'Music'; spatial composition of 13 textured and slit
woven cylinders; red, yellow,
black, white; 2.50m × 13–22
($8'2''$ × 5–$8\frac{3}{4}$)
Made by Ruta Bogustova,
Lithuania

163 – 'Untitled'; detail from one of a series of tapestries planned for a large public area. The whole dynamic effect depends on the juxtaposition of the individual optical patterns; 1.05m × 2.10m (3'5" × 6'10") Made by Kim Naver, Denmark

164 – 'Night'; textural details worked with a thicker yarn and an imaginative application of traditional techniques produce a three-dimensional effect (see detail); colour is also an important factor; handspun, natural shades of linen and wool; 2.30m × 1.15m (7'6½" × 3'9") Made by Berit Hjelholt, Denmark

Overpage

165 – 'Kultische Zelt'; slit and looped tapestry, linen and wool yarns; 3m × 1.80m (9'10" × 3'7½") Made by Susanne Hepfinger, West Germany

166 – 'Corner Piece'; this hard-edge tapestry was influenced by the 'shaped canvas' school of art Made by Archie Brennan, England

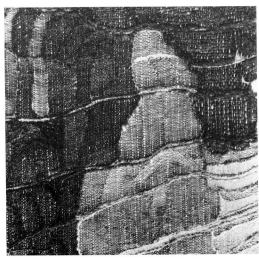

It is axiomatic that, given a painting and a weaving of equal size, the weaving will need to be surrounded by a greater area. The answer may well lie in the nature of fibre, each strand full, round, volumetric, charged with energy. Today's fibre art brightens architectural interiors just as historic tapestry added rich embellishment to medieval castles. Weavers have answered cold, over-tranquil surfaces of glass, steel, and terrazzo with the warm, sensorial, tactile lushness of fibre. Sheila Hicks,

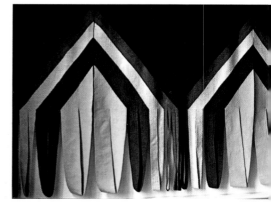

167 – 'Composizione Modulare' 1975; the continuous loop tabs are an interesting innovation to a traditional tapestry technique; 1.85m × 3.20m (6'2" × 10'6") Made by Sandra Marconato, Italy

168 – 'Tapisserie 1975'; mitered folds are worked on to the vertical surface; 2.60m × 2.55m (8'6" × 8'4½") Made by Judit Droppa, Hungary

169 – 'Exotica IV' 1975; wrapped sisal components on a haute-lisse background create a deeply textured surface, rich in shadows and highlights; cotton, raw silk, horse and goat hair; 2.60m × 1.90m (6'9" × 6'7") Made by Ritzi and Peter Jacobi, West Germany

170 – 'Raffia Basket' 1974;
knotted into irregularly faceted
surfaces, this piece is a fore-
runner of the artist's exploration
into the use of vinyl film for
knotting large volumes;
23 × 43 × 43 (9" × 17" × 17")
Made by Gary Trentham, USA

171 – 'Homage to Masae'; the
architectural character of this
piece that has the vertical
strength of many-lobed arches,
is an example of the artist's
free-standing, self-supporting
sculptures; red jute; 92 (36") high
Made by Claire Zeisler, USA

in sheer bravura performance, has led the way.
Unabashedly exuberant linen 'pony tails',
wrapped in brilliant silks, gush extravagantly
from the wall at the MGIC headquarters in
Milwaukee. In collaboration with the architect
Warren Platner, Hicks conceived textile walls
throughout all interiors with consistency and
harmony. She tends to use components
derived from one stage of the traditional Ikat
method: modular units of groups of threads,
compressed in cylinders by tight spot wrapping

172 – 'Five Rivers' 1974; large manila rope dyed in tones of blue to purple is the basic fibre for this braided structure, evoking the ebb and flow of the tributaries of a river; 2.60m × 3.30m wide (8' × 10') Made by Françoise Grossen, USA

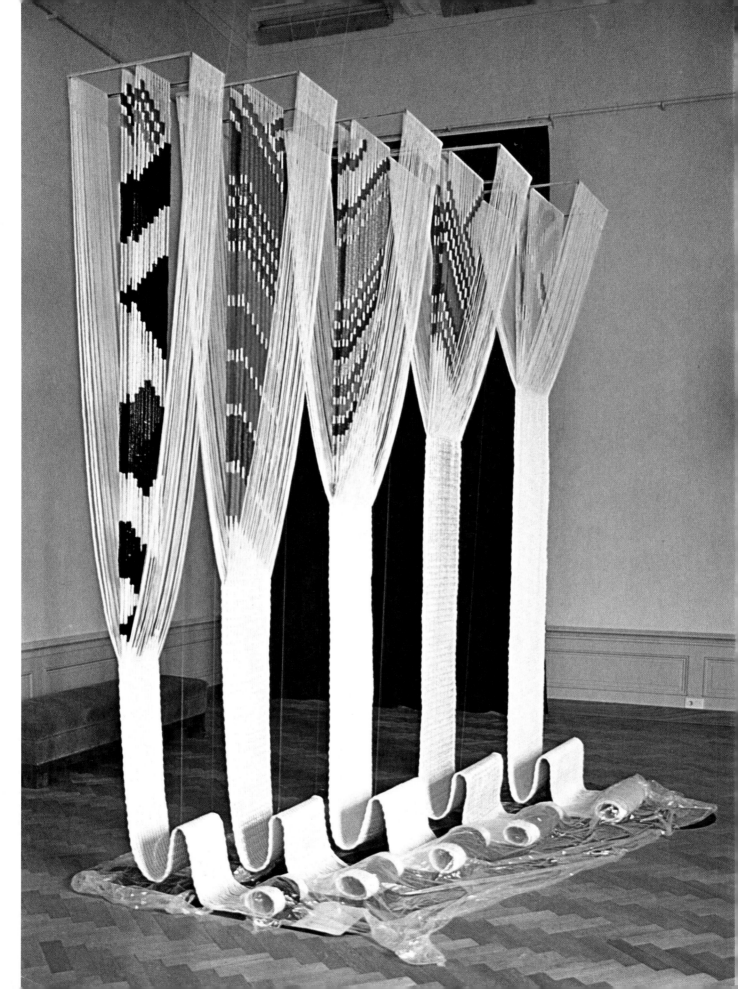

173 – 'Trinity, the Five Phantoms'
1974–75; a five part multi-level
weaving; suspended unwoven
warps are wrapped in a
controlled optical pattern;
4.50m × 2.80m × 1.80m
(14'7" × 9'2" × 5'11")
Made by Elsi Giauque,
Switzerland

174 – 'Fiber Wall' MGIC Headquarters, Milwaukee, 1973; the
entire wall is covered by
exuberant, brilliant cylinders
whose cores of yarn are periodi-
cally exposed; silk, wool;
wrapping technique
Made by Sheila Hicks, USA

175 – Detail

176 – 'The Unknown Garden'
1975; a simple motif is emphasized in pile then repeated in
reverse on the adjoining panel;
wool, linen; mixed technique
Made by Akiko Shimanuki,
Japan

that finally yield to spectacular flowing depths
of fibre. A rigorous intellectual control relates
seemingly random arrangements of these units
to an architectural pattern.

No less voluptuous are the undulating swags of
Japanese Masakazu Kobayashi. Of the
conviction that the sensuous curves of the
material are eloquent in themselves, he weaves
only a border to hold the work together.
Mihoko Matsumoto, a graduate of Cranbrook

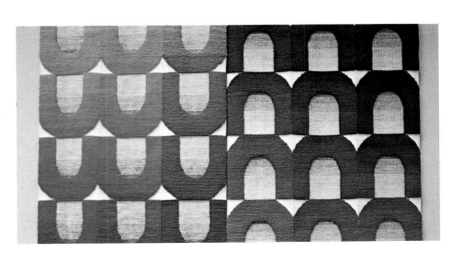

177 – 'Space-dyed Photographic
Weaving' 1975; the photographic
image on the sensitized woven
surface confers an opulent
quality to this piece;
2.44m × 3.66m × 30
(8' × 12' × 1')
Made by Lia Cook, USA

178 – 'Guernica' 1973; shaped
and assembled after weaving,
stable wefts control the
rigidity of interlaced tubes;
extensive deep pile treatment at
lower area contributes to the
gravitational 'pull';
2.35m × 1m × 90
(7'8" × 3'3" × 1')
Made by Joseph Grau-Garriga,
Spain

in Michigan but living in Japan, delineates
pattern by wrapping with colour and then
allows the cylindrical core to become exposed,
twisting around itself in three-dimensional
relief. Desirée Scholten of Holland celebrates
the yarn and its tonal values in a forthright,
uncomplicated palette spanning the spectrum
from white to red; the only weaving involved
is a supportive background over which fibres
float in chromatic dispersion. Akiko Shimanuki
of Japan emphasizes a simple motif, a Roman

arch, in deep colourful pile, then repeats it in reverse on a second adjoining panel. Lia Cook's weaving (California) is distinguished by massed, luxurious folds emanating seismic energy. The technique is loom-controlled; myriad white warps crowd into the loom reed to produce rep fabric; the weft is composed of irregular foam tubes hidden below the surface. Certain areas are then sensitized by photographic emulsion and exposed to an image; the result is panoramic. Lenore Tawney (United States) restrains colour in a deliberate attempt to enhance sculptural effect. Her weavings are at peace with the walls on which they are displayed, the meaning transmitted by deep values within their ritualistic symbolism. Freely suspended to be viewed in the round, her work maintains authentic presence that holds its own, yet does not compete with strong architecture.

180 – 'Magnet' 1974; the sensuous curves of the material are emphasized by tilting the composition forward; minimal weaving, only enough to hold the edges together; white cotton; 1.25m × 45 × 40 (4' × 1'6" × 1'4")
Made by Masakazu Kobayashi, Japan

181 – 'Tau' 1974; the cruciform image often recurring in this artist's work is expressed here in natural linen rep; 1.83m × 2.95m (6' × 9')
Made by Lenore Tawney, USA

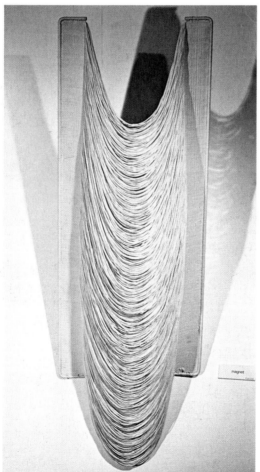

183 – Tapestry for the 'Zonnehuis' Sanatorium in Doorn, 1973; this serene tapestry is a celebration of those qualities of simplicity and discipline one associates with the East; the artist was in fact inspired by a favourite old Japanese painted screen; white cotton and polypropane; 1.35m × 2.40m (4'5" × 7'10")
Made by Wilhelmina Fruytier, Holland

182 – 'Images II'; the design of this piece is equally effective whether it is displayed horizontally or, as in the illustration, turned 90° from the way it was woven; weft flats on ribbed background; white linen
Made by Trude Guermonprez, USA

Another trend among textile artists who work architectonically is the repetition of a structural motif, that subordinates the fibre work to the qualities of light and space prevailing in situ, thus integrating the work and its surrounding into a harmonious whole. One of the most effective exponents of this approach is Moik Schiele who, by her own temperament and training, reflects Swiss pride in clearly ordered, uncompromising craftsmanship. Schiele understands the value of negative space, and

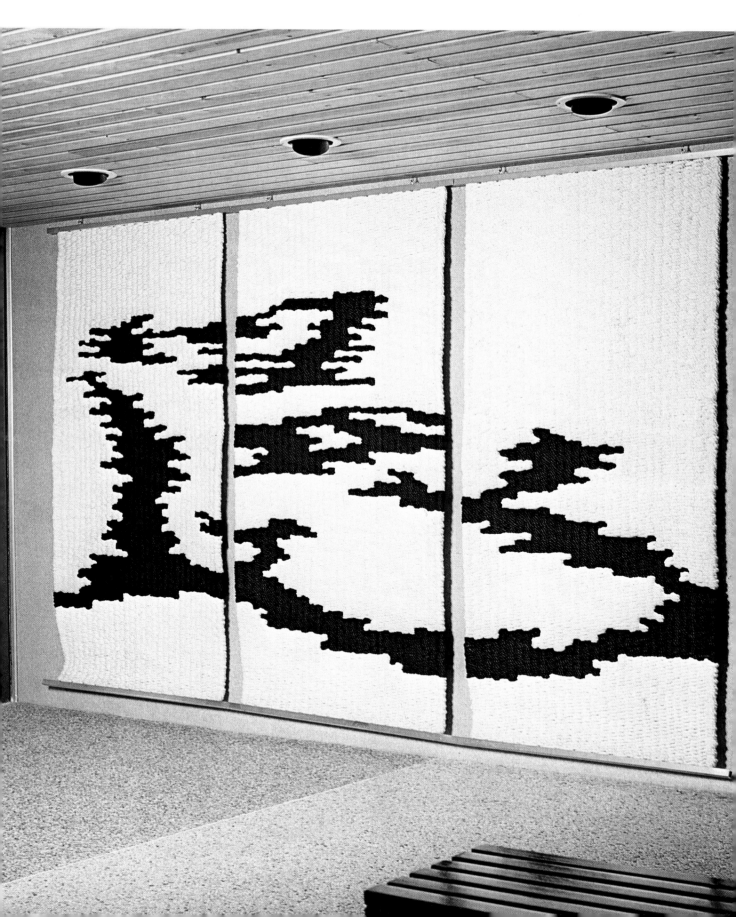

184 – 'Un Cerco de Adobe' 1971; the translation reads 'A Round Enclosure of Sun-baked Bricks'; natural wool and horse hair, mixed technique; 2.75m × 1.30m (9′ × 4′3″)
Made by Olga de Amaral, Colombia

185 – 'Copper Wave' for Glaubtern Church Centre, Neu-Affoltern, Switzerland, 1972; a counterpoint to the architectural elements, the slit tapestry has modulated curves of the same amplitude, but of a varying frequency; aluminium monofilament, mixed technique; 1.50m × 8m (4′7″ × 26′)
Made by Moik Schiele, Switzerland

186 – Detail from 'Room Element', showing how the depth of the curves is achieved by Schiele's method: two sets of warps are placed on two warp beams on the loom; one set of threads acts as a grid against which the longer waves of fibre flex at regular intervals

her insight exploits a regularly occurring phenomenon in tapestry: the slit, which happens where two colours abut. She weaves chaste, simple compositions of rectangles, generally neutral in tone, varying their size so as to maximize the opening. A sequential progression led her to similar pulsations on a regular frequency, waves that project from the slit surface, both frontal and obverse, in understated geometric reliefs. Technically more advanced, since the constant curving requires

differential tension, two sets of warps must be placed on two beams. To maintain sufficient rigidity to hold the curve, she has substituted wire for a fibre weft. The handsome work illustrated echoes structural relief in the large auditorium of Glaubtern Church Centre, Neu-Affoltern, Switzerland.

Weaving is also used as flexible architecture, as partitions and divisional boundaries. The woven walls of Olga de Amaral and the

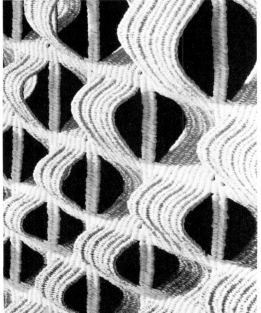

undulating volutes of Jagoda Buić (Jugoslavia)
are supreme examples. De Amaral is a petite
dynamo of energy. She directs a workshop
in Bogota that supplies her with wrapped
components and narrow strips; this reduces
for her the drudgery of production and
permits her to use her artistic skill to compose
with these units massive, mind-boggling walls
lavish with colour – not just rigid verticals but
swerving, swelling folds of fibre. Buić's walls are
tough sisal, often black, labyrinthine curves on

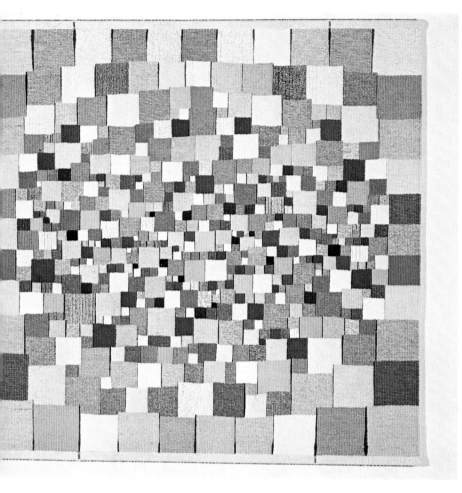

187 – 'Squares', 1966; the slits, occurring where two colours abut, imply a third dimension through their negative value; natural and synthetic fibres; 1.20m × 1.20m approximately (3'11" × 3'11")
Made by Moik Schiele, Switzerland

188 – 'Morning Glow' 1975; the pattern is delineated in wrapped cylinders with the cores becoming exposed and twisting around themselves in a three-dimensional relief; white cotton and silk; 1.90m × 2.30m (6'3" × 7'6")
Made by Matsumoto Mihoko, Japan

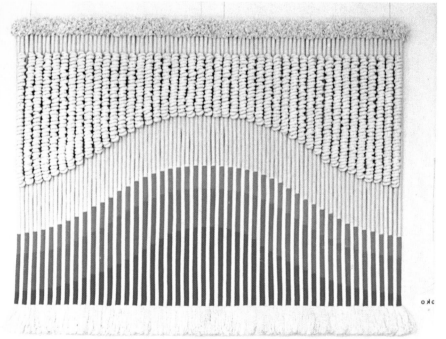

a massive scale. The characteristic herringbone that marks her work is applied with thick yarns. Able to stand alone, these tapestries literally replace walls.

The potential for using woven walls in architecture lies in collaboration between architect and weaver early in the planning stage, while lines are being drawn on paper. A successful example is Aurelia Muñoz's dramatic knotted column, suspended between floors

189 – 'Boog' 1973; the poetry
and symbolism of colours are
expressed fully in the tense
shape of this 'bow'; tapestry
technique, wool, sisal and plastic
fibres; 1.70m × 3.10m
(5'7" × 10'2")
Made by Herman Scholten,
Holland

190 – 'Rood' 1975; a celebration
of tonal values in a limited
palette; 'free' yarns in chromatic
progression are anchored on a
supportive woven background;
wool, cotton, sisal, linen, nylon,
rayon, plastic 3.10m × 1.70m
(10'2" × 5'7")
Made by Desirée Scholten,
Holland

191
'Of the Stone
Of the Sun
Of the Dream' 1975;
environmental tapestry; black
ribbed sisal; approximate height
2.50m (8'3")
Made by Jagoda Buić, Jugoslavia

Overpage

192 – 'Personaje en el Bosque' 1973;
knotted wall tapestry; natural
jute and sisal dyed by the artist;
2.78m × 2.78m (9'2" × 9'2")
Made by Aurelia Muñoz, Spain

of an industrial building in Barcelona.
Abakanowicz has defied architectural
conventions of walls in all but their loadbearing
function. Her environmental wall in the palatial
reception room of a new State Building in
's-Hertogenbosch, the Netherlands, grows
organically from floor to ceiling, 25' high along
a 71' span (see title page). Unprecedented in
scale and concept, the wall reasserts her
obsession with nature's irregular contours and
plant fibres. This tour de force consists of multi-

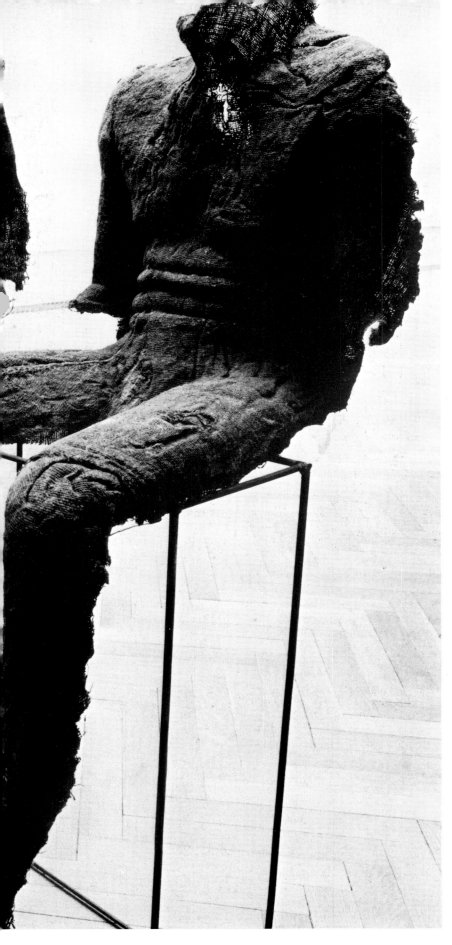

193 – 'Image de la Structure
Humaine' 1974–75; from the
cycle 'Altérations'; '. . . l'homme
appartient au monde des
structures organiques, à ses
rythmes et regles, contrairement
au monde artificial qu'il crée . . .';
burlap, jute and glue; personal
method; 1.50m × 6m
(4'11" × 19'8")
Made by Magdalena Abakanowicz,
Poland

panels, overlapped to create interplanar effect,
of earth-brown and black sisal, highlighted by
mauve and orange, relieved by crocheted
and knotted protrusions. The wall was largely
composed in situ by warping the vertical
surfaces and erecting a scaffold so that she
and her seven assistants could weave in place,
with direct involvement of fingers and hands
in the warp. Sensitively aware of the problems
confronting our society, Abakanowicz in her
latest work lashes out against pressures of the

competitive technological world, reflecting her compassionate misgivings for the individual who is the victim of systemization of life. In 'Alterations' she uses the humblest of fibre materials, burlap and jute combined with glue, to create some of her most disturbing work so far – a series of life-size truncated human figures seated in a row.

Liberation of attitude has elevated weaving from what was one of the minor applied arts to its deserved place in the curriculum of universities, and accounts for much of the change in approach. A student is now able to select fibre as the vehicle for creative expression with the same pride as he might choose paint or lithographic stone. The situation in an all art academy is even happier; there the weaver is subject to the discipline of the fine arts approach with the advantage that technique is not used restrictively, but as one of the possibilities for stating concept. As always, individual success depends on the insight to breach age-old tradition with the fresh winds of new thinking.

The prominent independent galleries of the world are dealing with fibre, some exclusively so. In New York André Emmerich accorded Olga de Amaral a one-woman exhibition of her fibre walls and structures; the Willard has managed Lenore Tawney (United States) with great éclat, and young Warren Hadler is intensely conscious of ascendant American fibre people; the Arras Gallery features Joseph Grau-Garriga. In Paris La Demeure, ahead of the scene, has for years exercised the discerning foresight to include Grau-Garriga, de Amaral, Jagoda Buić and Pierre Daquin (France). Private galleries in Kyoto and Tokyo show increasing affinity for Japanese textile artists, and it is well known that Japan has subsidized master craftsmen as Living National Treasures, holders of intangible cultural assets.

In 1976 the pace accelerated. In June the Handweavers Guild of America staged 'Fibre Structures' at the Carnegie-Mellon Museum of Art in Pittsburgh, 'a comparative analysis of utilitarian and non-utilitarian fiber structures'. The 'Nordic Textile Triennale' opened on July 1 at the handsome new museum by Alvar Aalto in Aalborg, Denmark, and circulated to Oslo, Malmo, Aabo, and Reykjavik. A second 'Miniature Textiles' event took place in Summer 1976 in London, while in the following Autumn the National Museum of Modern Art, Kyoto, presented 'Contemporary Fibre Works'.

Clearly, the future of fibre art portends more and better; this new form has only begun to be tapped. In an age when the individual is subject to so many pressures, it is reassuring to witness the potent upsurge of individual talent; when technological discoveries are used not to enrich our experience but to level out and debase spiritual values, it is particular significant that the artist should turn to simple organic fibres as means of expression, that he should find inspiration in old techniques preserved by small, comparatively isolated communities. Yet in this need to return to traditional sources lies the future of fibre art, its relevance and its strength.

Trends in Furnishing and Decorative Art

194 – 'Decibella'; system of sound and light screen. Each unit can be directed to particular areas to create 'acoustical caves' within large rooms without causing distortion; light can be directed down or upwards
Designed by Hans Westman for Westman-Atelieerna AB, Sweden

195 – 'Unfurling Flower' 1975; handmodelled porcelain; 14×9 ($5\frac{1}{2}'' \times 3\frac{1}{2}''$)
Made by Mary Rogers, England

196 – Desk: polished stainless steel; $2m \times 1m$ ($6'6\frac{3}{4}'' \times 3'3''$)
Designed by Ben Swildens for Point, France

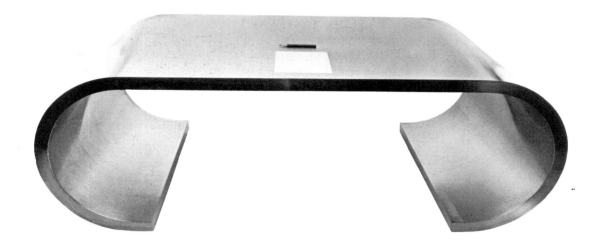

197, 198 – Dining table; can
expand from six to ten place
settings by inserting one or two
wedge-shaped leaves between
the two halves (see detail);
maple wood, laminated
construction
Made by Wendell Castle, USA

199 – GP 3 Centrepiece, orange,
white or grey ceramic;
36 × 55 × 9 (14″ × 21½″ × 3½″)
Designed by George Prudnikov
for Gabbianelli Spa, Italy

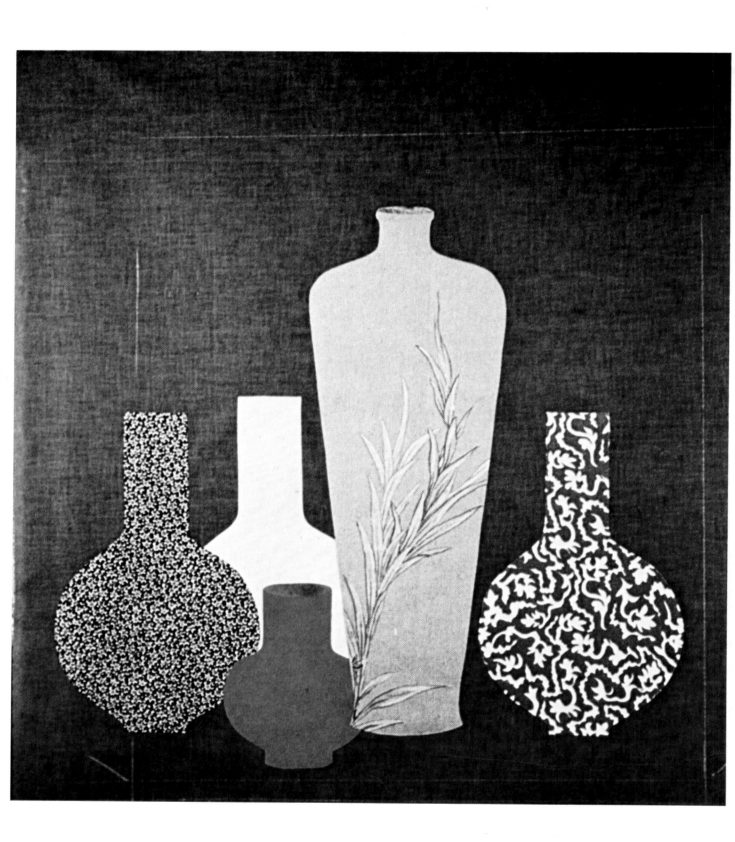

200 – Wall hanging
Made by S Murdoch, England

201 – Set of sterling silver
spoons, various sizes; hand
made by W. Phipps, England

202 – White porcelain pot,
cast, engraved, mono-fired;
about 15 (6") high
Made by Jacqui Poncelet,
England

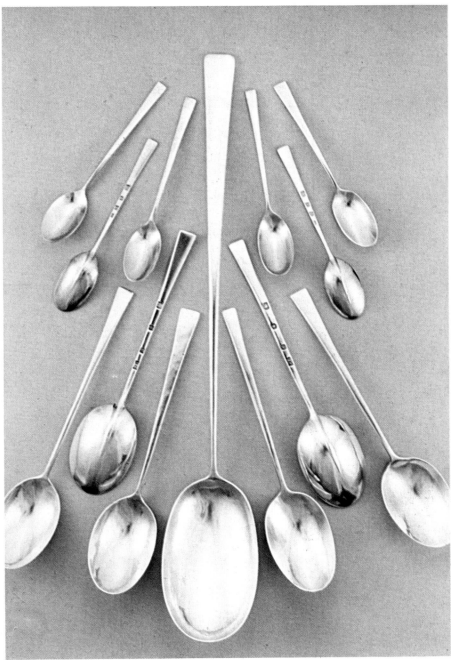

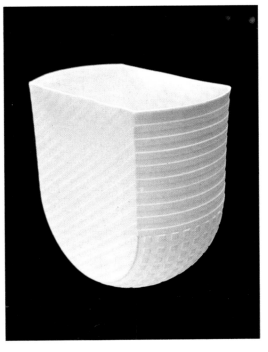

203 – Floor clock, oiled Brazilian
rosewood, glass, stainless steel;
175 × 45 × 30 (6'8" × 17¾" × 12")
Made by John Gaughan, USA

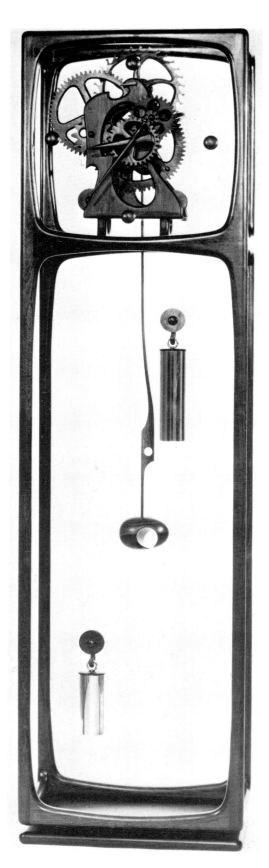

204 – 'Ash Chair 1975', tapered
lamination construction cane
seat and back;
Designed by Paul Haigh at the
Royal College of Art, England

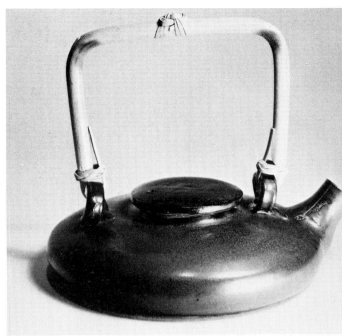

205 – Clay jar, 1969, American
Indian origin
S. Roberts Collection
*courtesy of the Museum of
Contemporary Crafts,* USA

206 – Teapot G207, stoneware
with grey glaze; 6 × 16.5 × 20.3
($2\frac{3}{8}''$ × $6\frac{1}{2}''$ × 8″)
Made by Ragnar Naess, USA

207 – 'Chest of Nine Drawers'
1975, a design of yew veneer
panels set into an Indian Laurel
frame with black line inlay;
the drawers are of mahogany
with cedar bottoms
Made by Martin Grierson,
England

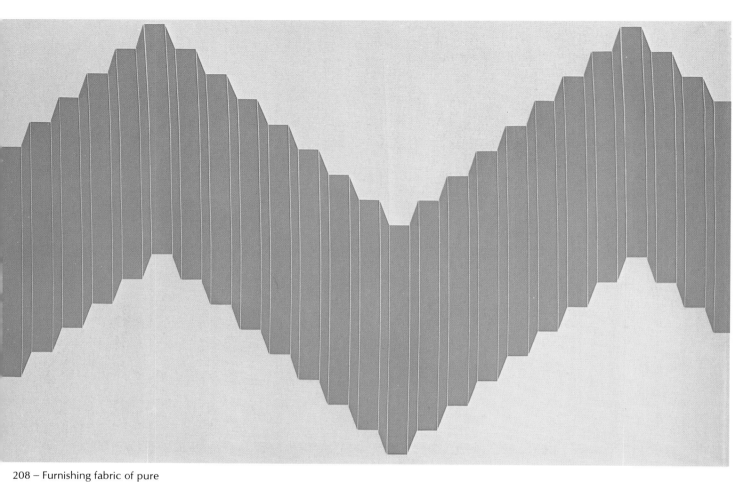

208 – Furnishing fabric of pure
cotton
Designed by Hiroshi Awatsuji
for Fujie Textile Co Ltd, Japan

209 – White pot with half foot;
cast bone china, hand modelled,
mono-fired; about 15 × 11
$(6'' \times 4\frac{1}{2}'')$
Made by Jacqui Poncelet,
England

210 – 'Lunario', coffee table;
pressed steel base (weighted),
oval or round top of wood,
lacquered white or black; a
taller, dining version is also
available
Designed by Cini Boeri for
Gavina, Italy

211 – 'Colonna' and 'Zigurrat',
ceramic containers
Designed by Sergio Asti for
Knoll International, USA

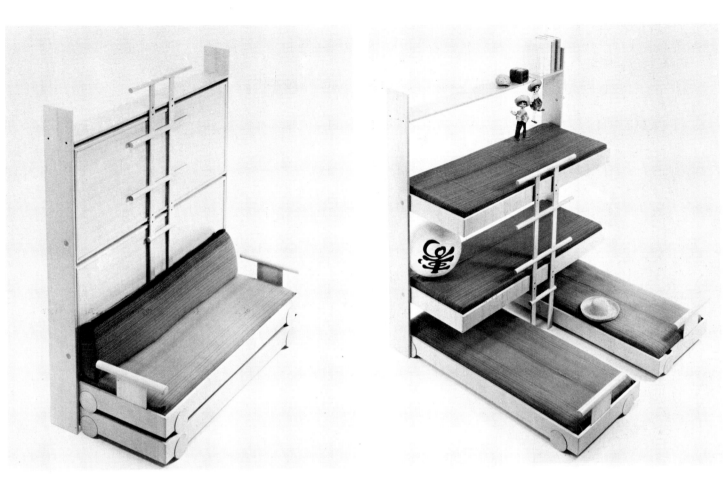

212, 213, 214 – Nest of four bunk
beds; two are hinged longi-
tudinally and can be pushed
against the wall when not used;
the other two fit within the
frame to become a sofa or be
pulled out at a 90° angle to
function as beds; natural ash,
2.40m × 2m × 75
(6'18½" × 6'6¾" × 2'6")
Designed and made by
Gigi Sabadin, Italy

215 – 'Pilato', wooden puppet
inspired by Dostoevsky's The
Inquisitor'; it is fully articulated
and made of variously coloured
unstained woods; 15 (6") tall
Made by Fernando Fara, Italy

216 – 'Madia', folding kitchen table for bread making
Designed by Arch. Panelli for Burelli Arredamenti, Italy

217 – Wooden bowl, pitch-pine; hand carved by Fabio Simion, Italy

218 – 'Tiki' cutlery set, a more slender variation of the 'Una' range; 18/8 stainless steel, satin finish, dishwasher proof
Designed by Tias Eckhoff for Norsk Stålpress A/S, Norway

219 – Containers for storing, cooking and eating food, of various sizes; stoneware, glazed inside
Made by John Leach, England

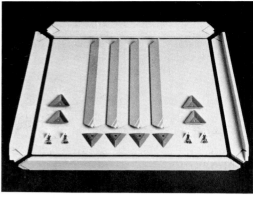

220 – Chair for self-assembly;
the plastic seat is fixed on four
metal rods, the backrest is
canvas
Designed by Enzo Mari for
Anonima Castelli, Italy

221, 222 – 'Table Range',
elements of various sizes are
assembled and held in position
by the triangular corner pieces
Designed by Paul Haigh at the
Royal College of Art, England

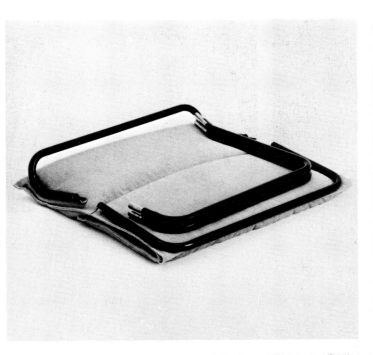

223, 224 – 'Taboga', collapsible chair in two sizes; lacquered steel tubing, stuffed and zipped canvas body
Designed and made by Arflex Spa, Italy

225 – 'Flaps' large armchair that converts into day bed or spare bed; polyurethane structure, Dacron filling
Designed by De Pas, D'Urbino, Lomazzi for Bonacina Srl, Italy

226, 227 – 'Orio', fluorescent
lamps; aluminium and Linestra,
50 (19½")
Designed by Sergio Mazza for
Quattrifolio, Italy

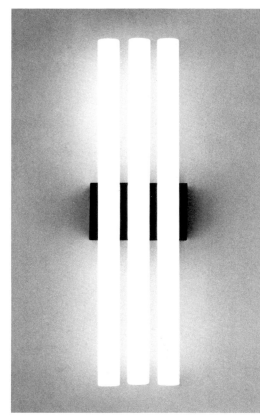

228 – Two bracelets and a
brooch 1975; silver inlaid with
blue and white resins
Made by Susanna Heron,
England

229 – 'Checkmate', sandblasted
decanters
Designed by Rolf Sinnemark for
Boda Bilder Ove Alström,
Sweden

230 – 'Pack', nomadic furniture;
the special canvas shell is
collapsible, the cushions are
polyurethane and Dacron with
a choice of covers; a two-place
sofa is also available
Designed by Alberto Rosselli
and Abe Kozo for Bonacina Srl,
Italy

231 – 'Sisten', lighting system of ten basic elements, can be assembled into 126 combinations of colours and materials Designed by Gianni Celata for Fontana Arte, Italy

232 – SL-544/23, coffee pot, 1976; sterling silver, hand made by Sigurd Persson, Sweden

233 – 'Aci' and 'Api', high fidelity electronic units; extruded aluminium and Perspex; Aci (pre-amplifier) is 3.2 ($1\frac{1}{4}$") high, Api (power amplifier) is 29.2 × 13.6 ($11\frac{1}{2}$" × $5\frac{3}{8}$") Designed by Robert Stuart and Allen Boothroyd for Lecson Audio Ltd England

234 – 'Phases of the Moon', stoneware plate set, 28 (11") diameter
Made by Audrey Bethel, USA

235 – Bowl, laminated birchwood turned on a lathe
Made by Rude Osolnik, USA

236 – 'Linda' chair, demountable frame, body composed of mortised wooden staves bent by steam; ash or walnut, 75 × 90 × 90 ($29\frac{1}{2}" \times 35\frac{1}{2}" \times 35\frac{1}{2}"$)
Designed by Roberto Toso and Roberto Pamjo for Stilwood Sas, Italy

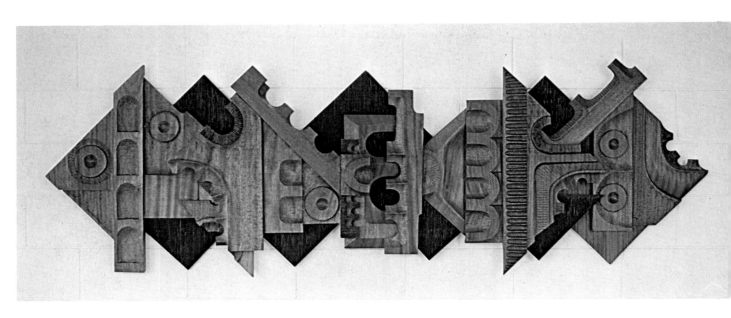

237 – 'Children of Tangaroa, God of the Sea', wall sculpture; stained and natural mahogany 2.36m × 91 (8' × 3') Carved by Fred Graham, New Zealand

238 – Three containers, unique pieces, blown glass Made by Pauline Solven, England

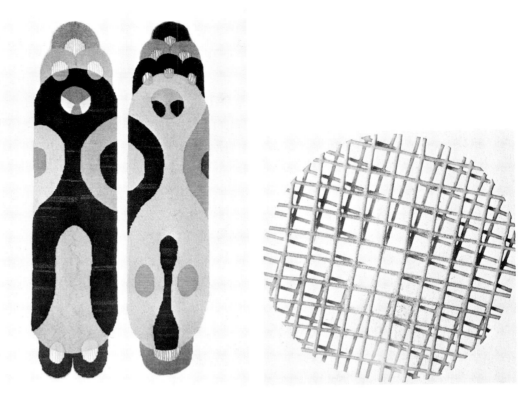

239 – 'Coupled Figures', hanging, tapestry technique
1.6m × 2.22m (3'6" × 7'6")
Made by Ruth Ginsberg-Place, USA

240 – Fruit holder; two superimposed grids of extruded majolica, pale white-grey glaze; about 50 (19½") diameter
Made by Alessio Tasca, Italy

241 – Folding gate leg table, veneered curl African mahogany framed in American black walnut; 1.50m × 1.10m (5' × 3'8")
Designed and hand-made by Martin Grierson, England

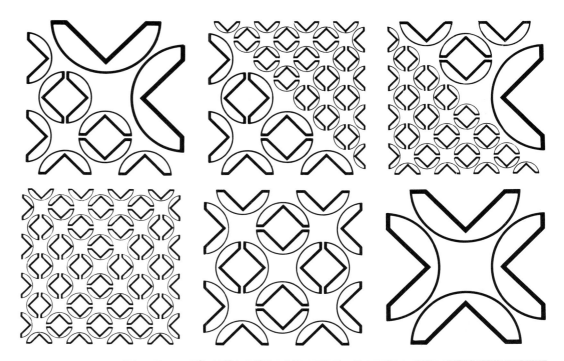

242 – Chair, black cherry and
cane; 1.22m × 91.5 × 53
(4′ × 3′ × 1′9″)
Made by William C. Leete, USA

243 – Display cabinet for small
objects, moulded and laminated
Perspex and aluminium;
62 (24½″) high
Designed by Elizabeth Lecky
for John Green, England

244 – Six graphics for silk-screen
printed tiles; 25 × 25
(9⅞″ × 9⅞″)
Designed by Nino Caruso for
Ceramiche Matteo d'Agostino,
Italy

245 – Ceramic containers, white
or black;
Designed by Sergio Asti for
Knoll International, USA

246 – Necklace, silver and
carved ivory
Made by Caroline Broadhead,
England

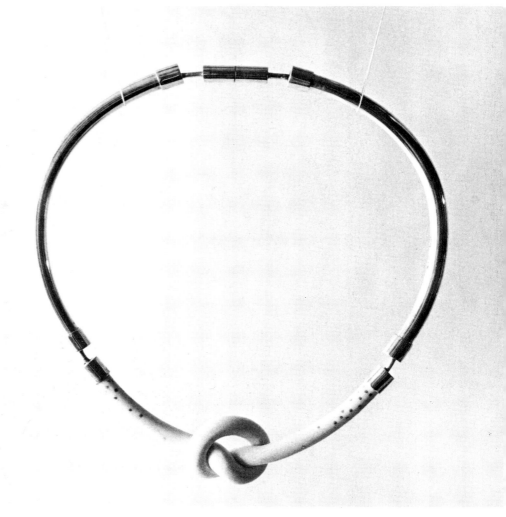

247 – 'Ariadne' 1975; unique
piece; blown glass, 15 × 15
(6" × 6")
Made by Sigurd Persson for
Kosta Glasbruk, Sweden

248 – Hinged broken brooch
and pair of broken brooches,
ivory and silver; 5 × 5 (2″ × 2″)
approximately
Made by Caroline Broadhead,
England

249 – 'Gyro' 1975 bracelet,
18ct gold and white acrylic
Made by David Watkins, England

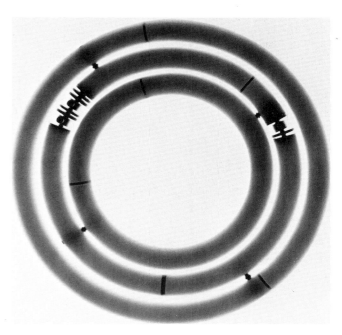

250 – 'Feather Lady' 1971,
brooch; sterling silver/fire gilt
plastic enamel, parrot feathers;
13.5 × 13.5 (5¼″ × 5¼″)
approximately
Made by Arline M. Fisch, USA

251 – 'Spring Chair No. 1' 1973,
laminated ash construction;
sling of layered canvas, leather
and cotton; 1.37m × 91.5 × 76
(4'6" × 33" × 30")
Made by William C. Leete, USA

252 – 'Polo', office chair; fully
adjustable and rotating metal
structure with expanded
polyurethane seat, can be
fitted with arm and footrests;
white, yellow, blue or green
Designed by Paolo Parigi for
Heron Parigi, Italy

253 – 'Waldorf', ceramic
containers, black or white
Designed by Sergio Asti for
Knoll International, USA

254 – 'Heron Delta', precision
drawing table; steel sprayed
white with black finish
Designed by Paolo Parigi for
Heron Parigi, Italy

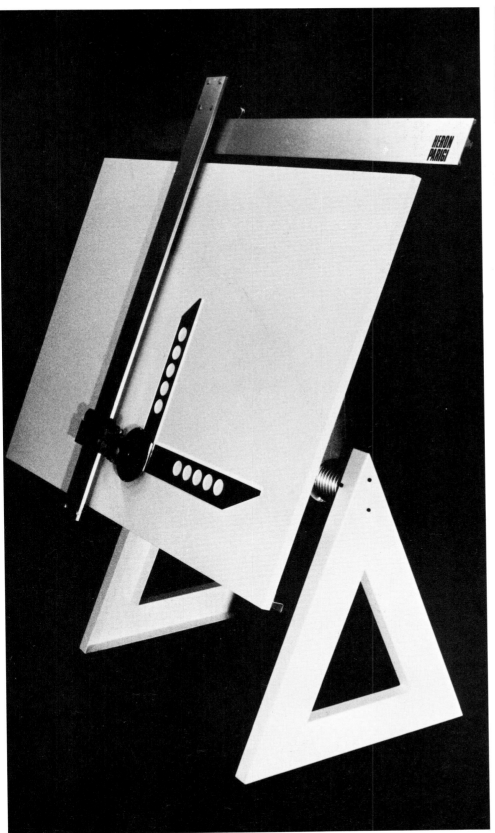

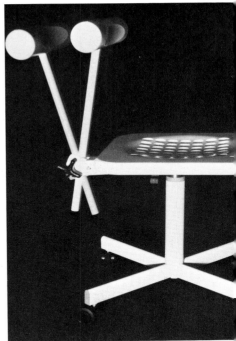

255, 256, 257, 258 – Chairs, from the '2100 Thonet-Flex' range, assembled from three main interchangeable elements; the exceptional versatility of this design results from a synthesis of function, material and manufacturing techniques. A plastic shell rests on two sturdy wooden H frames; chairs can be linked together or to various accessories to the range. If the wooden elements are changed over and the frames face inwards, a narrower and lighter looking individual chair is obtained. Black plastic shell or with optional upholstery, beech frame, clear varnished or stained red, green or brown Designed by Gerd Lange for Gebrüder Thonet AG, West Germany

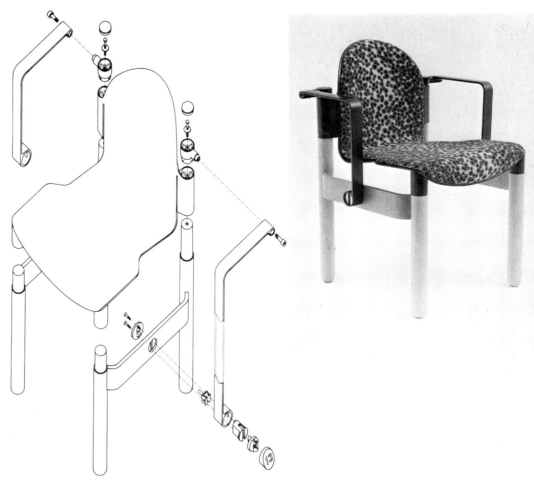

259 – 'Mechanical Glass Graphic',
lead channel, ridged clear glass,
opaque glass, mirror, wood;
86 (34¾") high
Made by Richard Millard, USA

260 – Chair No. 78; teak or
rosewood, seat of woven flax
or woolweb, fabric, paper cord,
plastic or natural leather
Designed by N. O. Møller for
J. L. Møller Møbelfabrik,
Denmark

261 – Food trolley for self-
assembly; injection moulded
metacrilate, black, white or red
structure, white trays;
64 × 60 × 13.5
($25\frac{1}{4}''$ × $23\frac{1}{2}''$ × $5\frac{1}{2}''$)
Designed by Luigi Massoni for
Fratelli Guzzini, Italy

262 – 'Opalin' candleholder,
white glass, 21 (8¼")
Designed by F. Meydam for
Royal Leerdam Glasfabriek,
Holland

263 – S39 candleholder, blown
glass and silver plate;
28 × 8 × 16 (11" × 3⅛" × 6¼")
Designed by Lino Sabattini for
Sabattini Argenteria, Italy

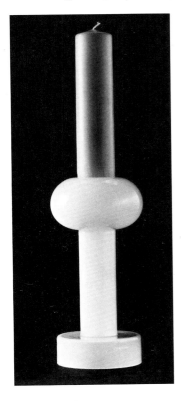

264 – From the 'Gourmet
Series' cutlery: sardine fork,
snail fork and tongs, lobster
fork, crab fork and knife,
oyster fork; 18/8 steel, 90 g
Alpaca silver plated or solid
silver
Designed by Carl Pott for
C. Hugo Pott, West Germany

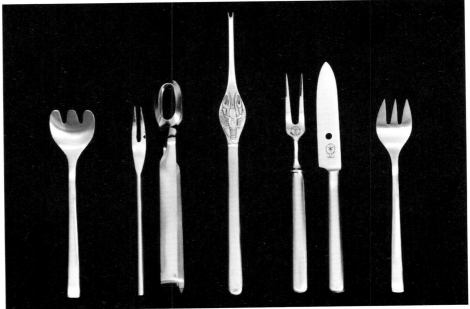

265 – 'Windowpiece I', 1976; the cloud form is solid lead crystal on window glass previously sandblasted with the cube image; 60 × 80 (23½″ × 31½″)
Designed by Ann Wärff for Kosta Boda, Sweden

266 – 'Teapot sculpture' 1975, bas-relief; sandblasted form encased in clear crystal; 20 (8″) high
Designed by Ann Wärff for Kosta Boda, Sweden

267 – 'Sculpture' 1976, solid clear and sandblasted crystal; 30 (11¾″) high
Designed by Ann Wärff for Kosta Boda, Sweden

268 – 'Sculpture with a Flower'
1976, sandblasted form encased in
clear and sandblasted crystal;
45 (17¾") high
Designed by Ann Wärff for
Kosta Boda, Sweden

269 – 'Windowpiece II', 1976;
solid crystal in sandblasted
window glass; 60 × 80
(23" × 31½")
Designed by Ann Wärff for
Kosta Boda, Sweden

270 – 'Glass Landscape 1976';
mould blown multicoloured
glass, hot tooled trees, slip cast
hand-painted house
Made by Jane Bruce, England

271 – 'Panel 1974'; porcelain
with green glaze; 30.5 × 30.5
(12″ × 12″)
Made by Eileen Lewenstein,
England

272 – Stoneware pot with a flat
lip; wheel thrown, hand built,
pale green glaze
Made by Hans Coper, England

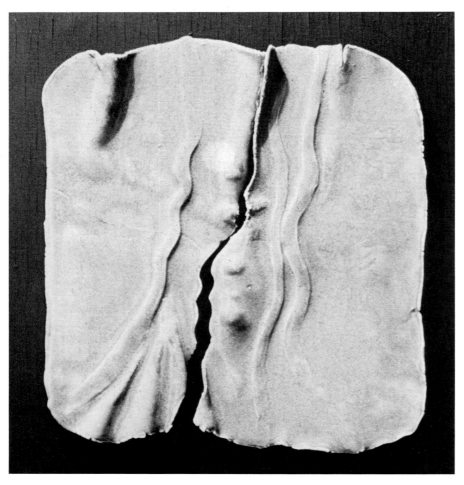

273 – 'Ophelia-Opening-Night',
stoneware lidded container with
Chinese tassels, beads, wax-resist
glaze decoration; 23 (9") high
Made by William Wilhelmi, USA

274 – 'Moon Pocket', stoneware
pot with slip finish; 23 × 9
(9" × 3½")
Made by Lizzie Fritsch, England

75 – 'Wessex Nightfall', crystal bowl engraved by Laurence Whistler, England

276 – White Opal Form, 1973; freehand tooled glass, unique piece; 33 (13") high
Made by Joel Philip Myers, USA

277 – 'Optical bottle 1975';
stoneware, hand built and
painted with slip; 25 (10") high
Made by Elizabeth Fritsch,
England

278 – 'Split form with a
hemisphere 1975'; white bone
china cast and polished after the
bisque firing, unglazed
Made by Jacqueline Poncelet,
England

279 – 'Necklace 1973'; ring knit
construction, fine silver wire,
sterling silver with blue and
green antique glass finials; 30.5
(12") long
Made by Arline Fisch, USA

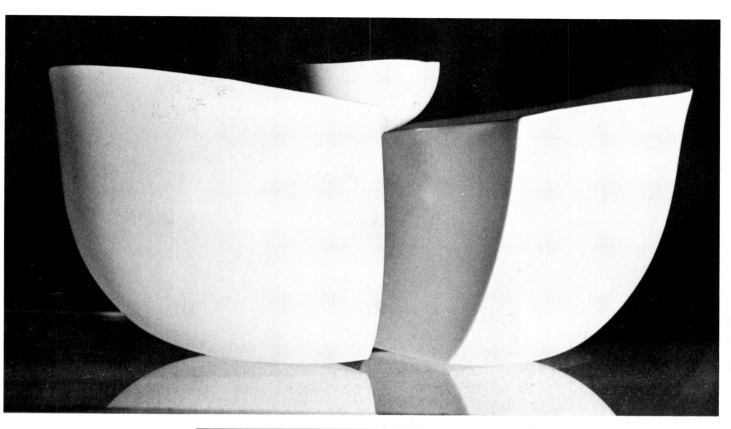

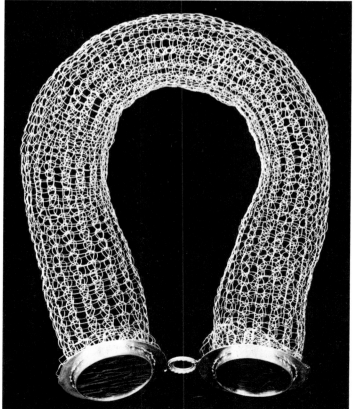

Overpage

280 – Drinks cabinet, Rio
rosewood with sycamore inlays;
1.37m (4'6") high
Made by David Field, England

281 – Necklace, acrylic and gold
Made by David Watkins,
England

282 – Set of rings on acrylic stand
Made by Wendy Ramshaw,
England

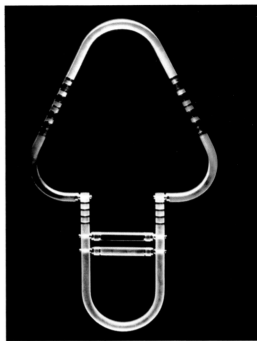

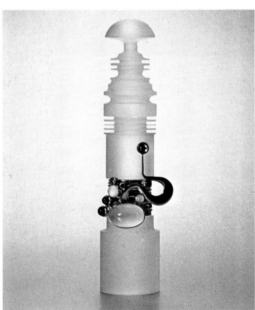

283 – 'Work I', silk kimono; the purple weft, dip-dyed before weaving with 'Shikon', a vegetable dye, passes through the light-coloured warp that includes an area of varying numbers of threads in order to produce the precise, vertical bands of different shades; Designed, hand-woven and made by Fukumi Shimura, Japan
Courtesy of The National Museum of Modern Art, Kyoto

Manufacturers and Designers

Magdalena Abakanowicz
Al. Stanow Zjednoczonych 16/53
Warsaw
Poland

Ceramiche Matteo d'Agostino
Salerno
Italy

Olga de Amaral
Calle 72 no.10/61
Bogotà
Colombia

Arflex Spa
via Monte Rosa 27
20051 Limbiate (Milano)
Italy

Audrey Bethel
5514 Howe Street
Pittsburgh, Pa 15232
USA

Boda Bilder Ove Alström
Box 134
36065 Boda Glasbruk
Sweden

Corrie de Boer
Frans van Mierisstraat 135
Amsterdam
Holland

Ruta Bogustova
226059 Riga
Vaidavas 13/58
USSR

Bonacina Srl
viale Brianza 30
Meda
Italy

Cyril Bourquin-Walfard
26 Porte-de-Pully
CH-1009 Pully
Switzerland

Jagoda Buić
c/o Marković
11000 Beograd
3 Dositejeva
Jugoslavia

Archie Brennan
c/o BCC
43 Earlham Street
London WC2
England

Caroline Broadhead
5 Dryden Street
London WC2
England

Jane Bruce
c/o The Glasshouse
27 Neal Street
London WC
England

Burelli Arredamenti
33010 Feletto (Udine)
Italy

Anomina Castelli Spa
via Torreggiani 1
40126 Bologna
Italy

Wendell Castle
18 Maple Street
Scottsville NY 14546
USA

Lia Cook
1438 Grove Street
Berkeley, Cal 94709
USA

Hans Coper
c/o CAC 12 Waterloo Place
London SW1
England

Judit Droppa
Lóránt út 27
1125 Budapest
Hungary

David Field
5 Dryden Street
London WC2
England

Fernando Fara
c/o Carla Caccia
via Boccaccio 16
Milano
Italy

Arline M Fisch
4316 Arcadia Drive
San Diego, Cal 92103
USA

Fontana Arte Spa
Alzaia Trieste 59
20094 Corsico (Milano)
Italy

Lizzie Fritsch
c/o CAC
12 Waterloo Place
London SW1
England

Wilhelmina Fruytier
Amsteldijk-n 168
Ouderkerk A/D
Amstel
Holland

Fujie Textile Co Ltd
7, 12, 4-chome
Sendagaya
Shibuya-ku
Tokyo

Gabbianelli Spa
via Pallanza 6
20125 Milano
Italy

John Gaughan
5223 San Fernando Road W,
Los Angeles, Cal 90039
USA

Elsi Giauque
Festi
2514 Ligerz
Switzerland

Ruth Ginsberg-Place
157 Warren Avenue
Boston, Mass 02116
USA

Daniel Graffin
5 rue Larrey
75005 Paris
France

Fred Graham
36 Kelvyn Grove
Manurewa
Auckland
New Zealand

José Grau-Garriga
c/o Virginia West
'Westwood' RFD no. 7
Baltimore, Maryland 21208
USA

Martin Grierson
5 Dryden Street
London WC2
England

Trude Guermonprez
c/o Virginia West
'Westwood' RFD no. 7
Baltimore, Md 21208
USA

Fratelli Guzzini
62019 Recanati (Macerata)
Italy

Susanne Hepfinger
Thierschstrasse 1
8000 München 22
West Germany

Susanna Heron
c/o CAC
12 Waterloo Place
London SW1
England

Heron Parigi
PO Box 13
50032 Borgo S Lorenzo (Firenze)
Italy

Sheila Hicks
30 rue Dauphine
75006 Paris
France

Berit Hjelholt
c/o Virginia West
'Westwood' RFD no. 7
Baltimore, Md 21208
USA

Ritzi and Peter Jacobi
Hartheimerstrasse 6
7131 Neubärental
West Germany

Knoll International
320 Park Avenue
New York NY 10020
USA

Kobayashi Masakazu
32 Nakabayashi-cho
Shugakuin
Sakyo-ku
Kyoto
Japan

Kosta Boda
Kosta
Sweden

John Leach
Muchelney Pottery
Muchelney, nr Langford
Somerset
England

Lecson Audio Ltd
St Ives, Huntingdonshire
England

Royal Leerdam Glassworks
PO Box 8
Leerdam
Holland

William C Leete
Art and Design Dept.
Northern Mich University
Marquette, Mich 49855
USA

Eileen Lewenstein
11 Western Esplanade
Hove
Sussex BN4 1WE
England

Sandra Marconato
via Fratelli Bandiera 6
Padova
Italy

Matsumoto Mihoko
1813–5 Shiromachi
Yamato Koriyama-shi
Nara Prefecture
Japan

Richard Millard
111 East 26th Street
New York NY 10010
USA

Aurelia Muñoz
Av. José Antonio 586
Barcelona 11
Spain

S Murdoch
c/o CAC
12 Waterloo Place
London SW1
England

Joel Philip Myers
RR2, Bunn Street Road
Bloomington, Ill 61701
USA

Ragnar Naess
North River Pottery
107 Hall Street
Brooklyn NY 11205
USA

Kim Naver
c/o Virginia West
'Westwood' RFD no. 7
Baltimore, Md 21208
USA

Norsk Stalpress S/A
Breiviken 10
PO Box 3440
5001 Bergen
Norway

Rude Osolnik
2320 CPO
Berea, Ky 40403
USA

Sigurd Persson
Höbergsgatan 11
11645 Stockholm
Sweden

W Phipps
c/o CAC
12 Waterloo Place
London SW1
England

Jacqui Poncelet
c/o CAC
12 Waterloo Place
London SW1
England

C Hugo Pott
Ritterstrasse 28
D-5650 Solingen
West Germany

Quattrifolio Sas
Corso Monforte
20122 Milano
Italy

Wendy Ramshaw
c/o CAC
12 Waterloo Place
London SW1
England

Mary Rogers
Brook Farmhouse
Nanpantan Road
Loughborough
England

Royal College of Arts
Kensington Gore
London SW7
England

Gigi Sabadin & Co Snc
Romano D'Ezzelino (Vicenza)
Italy

Sabattini Argenteria
via A Volta
22072 Bregnano (Como)
Italy

Moik Schiele
Rennweg 7
8001 Zurich
Switzerland

Shimanuki Akiko
3–402 Mita 3–1–2
Tama-ku
Kawasaki-shi
Kanagawa Prefecture
Japan

Fukumi Shimura
c/o The National Museum
of Modern Art
Okazaki, Sakyo-ku
Kyoto
Japan

Desirée and Herman Scholten
Kleiweg 32 B
Baambrugge
Holland

Fabio Simion
c/o Carla Caccia
via Boccaccio 16
Milano

Liselotte Siegfried
Sempacherstrasse 14
8032 Zurich
Switzerland

Pauline Solven
Ravenshill
Cliffords Mesne
Newent, Glo's
England

Stilwood Sas
41032 Cavezzo (Modena)
Italy

Ben Swildens
67 rue de l'Université
Paris
France

Alessio Tasca Ceramiche
via Roberti 15
36055 Nove (Vicenza)
Italy

Lenore Tawney
64 Wooster Street
New York NY 10012
USA

Gebrüder Thonet A/G
3558 Frankenberg
Michael-Thonet-Strasse
West Germany

Gary Trentham
241 Green Street
Auburn, Alabama
USA

David Watkins
c/o CAC
12 Waterloo Place
London SW1
England

Westman-Atelieerna A/B
Lund
Sweden

Laurence Whistler
Little Place
Lyme Regis
Dorset
England

William Wilhelmi
1129 Ocean Drive
Corpus Christi, Tx 78404
USA

Claire Zeisler
230 E. Ohio
Chicago 60611
USA